THE SPORTS CAR

THE SPORTS CAR

IAN WARD

photography
Jasper Spencer-Smith

BLANDFORD PRESS
Poole　　　　Dorset

First Published in the U.K. 1982 by Blandford Press.
Link House, West Street,
Poole, Dorset, BH15 1LL

Copyright © 1982 Blandford Books Ltd

Distributed in the United States by
Sterling Publishing Co., Inc.,
2 Park Avenue, New York, N.Y. 10016.

British Library Cataloguing in Publication Data

Ward, Ian
   The sports car.
   1. Sports car — History
   I. Title
   629.22′22   TL236

ISBN 0 7137 1072 1

Typeset by Keyspools Ltd, Golborne, Lancs, U.K.
Printed in Singapore

CONTENTS

INTRODUCTION

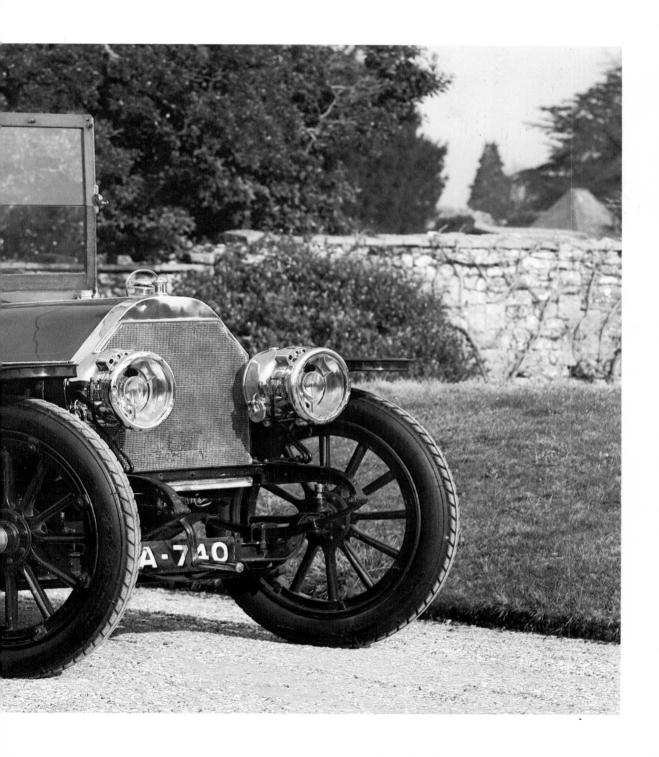

What is a sports car? We all know in our own minds whether a certain car has a sporting character or not, but it is very difficult to formulate a definition which will encompass all the vehicles that have been accepted as sporting machines.

In the early part of the century, an attempt was made to define the breed and according to that description a sports car is one which cannot be entered by a gentleman without his first either stooping or removing his top hat. However, it is not surprising that ideas were so vague and ludicrous, as it was not until 1919 that the words 'sports car' were first coined in an article in *The Autocar*. Not that matters had improved greatly some forty years later: an American text of 1960 decided that a sports car had to be equipped with front seats that did not fold down to form beds.

It is easy to say that all sports cars must have no more than two seats, but this is patently untrue, because there have been many fine sports cars, such as the Vauxhall 'Prince Henry' and the Le Mans Bentleys, which have had at least four seats. Equally, there have been plenty of two-seaters which could hardly be described as sporting. Neither does weight provide the answer: although most sports cars are lighter than their saloon counterparts, there have been some massive examples which have overcome their weight penalty by being equipped with a suitably large engine. Similarly, the motoring years have produced some lightweight saloons which have nothing more in their favour than their low mass. Perhaps all sports cars have folding hoods? This premise falls down even before the words have been uttered, as in the early days of motoring the majority of cars were open and in recent years very few, sporting or otherwise, have offered the joys of fresh-air motoring to their occupants. What of speed? Even this does not provide us with the answer, for a great many sports cars have actually been slower than other machines which are most definitely non-sporting.

Previous page : widely regarded as the daddy of them all – the Mercédès 60 hp of 1903, one of which, substituted for the 90 hp racers destroyed by fire, won the Gordon Bennett event of that year.

Perhaps the most satisfactory solution to this dilemma comes in a description put forward by the eminent motoring historian Cyril Posthumus some years ago. He suggested that a sports car was one in which performance took precedence over appointment. There are very few, if any, exceptions to this rule and it applies to sports tourers as well as to outright performance cars. The sports tourer is certainly a slightly different animal from the purpose-built sportster, but we are once again faced with some difficulty in drawing a line between the two. In general the sports tourer combines the speed and agility of its cousin with a certain degree of sophistication and luxury and, in most cases, greater seating capacity.

In the early days it was largely the open top of the sports tourer that distinguished it from its more mundane counterparts. The 'Grand Tour' was a fine way for the well-to-do to pass a pleasant time during the summer months each year, perhaps driving around the warm climes of the Mediterranean coasts for a few weeks. For this purpose, what better than a luxurious open-topped car, offering grace and comfort combined with discreet but adequate performance. More recently, the Grand Tourer title, abbreviated to its initial letters, has come to be applied to many types of motor car, some with neither sporting nor luxurious pretensions and others which are hardly practicable for the road and which would certainly not offer the means of a stylish holiday. Indeed, modern times have bred a new type of GT machine, which in many cases has ousted the true sports car by offering the wherewithal to impress either neighbours or friends – in the form of stripes, wide wheels, special seats, etc – without the superfluous luxuries such as more power, better brakes and so on. It is easy for a driver to convince himself that he has improved his car's performance simply by fitting a 'sports' silencer or a quick-acting throttle pedal; in fact he might as well have the speedometer re-calibrated for all the good that such modifications do.

The 'boy-racer' mentality is not entirely new: throughout motoring history there has been a healthy market for 'different' versions of mundane cars. At the outset, when car development was in its infancy, there were plenty of ingenious owners who set about modifying their own cars. Indeed, this is how many new makes sprang into being, the modified machines attracting more interest than the standard item. In most cases of this type, there has been a minimum – or perhaps a complete lack – of mechanical alteration and the car has possibly had embarrassingly little power together with downright dangerous road manners, but to its driver it has felt like a completely different machine from the original. There is no doubt that looks play an all-important part in formulating a driver's opinion of the sporting capabilities of a motor car.

When the motor industry was finding its feet – and indeed right up to the outbreak of World War II – it was common for manufacturers large and small to offer their products in chassis form to be clothed by one of the multitude of specialist coachbuilders. As time progressed there was usually at least one standard body, but it was nevertheless the outside stylists who were largely responsible for determining the type and character of a car. So it might well be that a chassis intended as nothing more than a straightforward family car by its manufacturer would be turned into a sleek, attractive sports car by its tailor. After all, it was in this way that the MG name was born. Cecil Kimber decided that he could improve the products of William Morris by fitting new coachwork and motoring enthusiasts were quick to agree.

So where did the sports car begin its career? It has often been said that in the beginning all cars were sports cars: as we have seen, most were open topped, in fact few offered any form of weather protection to the occupants, and many had only two seats. It is certainly true that the owner of an early motor car needed to be something of a sportsman, as reliability generally left a great deal to be desired and there was hardly a network of service agents available to carry out repairs. In many cases the rectification of faults was a case of make do and mend, village blacksmiths suddenly finding themselves thrust into a completely new world. Vehicles such as these, however, are sports cars only to the cynics who like to ridicule the efforts of the pioneer manufacturers and owners. Although few machines offered a great degree of luxury, neither was performance a major consideration – they were just cars.

It was man's natural competitive spirit which paved the way for the sports car towards the end of the nineteenth century. Reliability trials began to take place, in which the idea was to finish an arduous course rather than to arrive first. It was not long, however, before these developed into proper races, usually over enormous distances on the appalling roads of the day and generally centred on Paris. The primitive cars became even cruder, as the leading manufacturers pared weights to a minimum and fitted ever larger power units. These moves certainly gave some of the machines extremely impressive speed capabilities, but little or no thought was ever given to how well a car would corner or stop and, as a result, accidents were legion. Despite the problems, lessons were learned and competition experience began to improve the breeds. Apart from satisfying man's desire to beat his fellow, these events were also providing highly desirable publicity for those makers whose cars did well – in fact, any car which finished intact could be considered to have done well.

In the opening years of this century, sophistication began to find a place and the racing cars took on more of an air of practicality. This allowed their builders to offer replicas, as in the case of Austin with a Grand Prix replica of 1908. Many of the early sports cars, then, were based on competition cars of the period, but strangely the machine accepted as the first sports car was never intended for racing. This was the Mercédès 60 hp of 1903, which was constructed purely for road use and was only forced into competition when the team racers were destroyed by fire. It featured such niceties as a gate gearchange and a proper honeycomb radiator (in place of the fore-and-aft change and the gilled tube cooler) and it set the style for the future.

Many of the best early sports cars came out of the Herkomer and Prince Henry Trials; in fact several such machines were named after the latter. More notable among these were the fine Vauxhall Prince Henry, which developed into the famous 30/98, and Dr Porsche's Prince Henry Austro-Daimler.

The end of World War I brought new technical advances to the motor industry as spin-offs from aviation. New materials, such as light alloys for pistons, became available and a better understanding of engine balancing, together with improved bearings, opened the way for higher crankshaft speeds. In the 1920s, the sports car began to develop more surely in its own right, being less dependent either on its saloon cousins or on those of the race track. This is not to say, however, that there was no longer any place for the road-going sportster in competition: trials were becoming ever more popular and the likes of Bentley were really showing the way at Le Mans with large sports tourers.

The 1920s also saw the emergence of a new kind of light car to replace the rather unpleasant cyclecars which had gone before. At the forefront of this trend was the Austin Seven. This was basically a family car but was soon to become available in a wealth of sporting forms, both official and unofficial. Indeed, the Austin Seven provided the most popular base for specials for many years.

In the 1930s style and comfort began to find more of a place in the sporting field and some of the most famous sporting names came into the limelight: Frazer Nash, Aston Martin, Delage and Delahaye, HRG, BMW and SS-Jaguar are only a few, but they offer a taste of those heady pre-war days. Once again, war brought great advances in motoring technology, but this time there was a long post-war period of austerity and it was not until the 1950s that new ideas really began to oust the old from favour. In sports racing, the 1950s belonged to Jaguar, whose C- and D-types swept all before them to take five Le Mans victories. The company's racing prowess was reflected in the ubiquitous XK series of sports cars which offered so much performance for so little money.

In the next decade the sports car, as a hairy beast, had passed its prime: legislation, particularly in America, and a desire for more creature comforts, were killing off the convertibles and bringing in their place a new type of fast saloon or closed coupé. It became fashionable to own a Lotus-Cortina or a Mini-Cooper and few seemed to notice that we were losing the likes of the Austin-Healey 3000. There were still some fine sports machines, but as the 1970s progressed these seemed to move steadily up market and further out of reach of the average enthusiast. With the dawn of the 1980s there

came whispers of new convertibles from companies such as Jaguar and Lotus, but otherwise the convertible sports field belonged to Triumph, with the soon-to-die TR7, and to a few hardy specialist concerns.

The sports car has a long and distinguished career behind it; hopefully the wheel is about to turn full circle, so that the next few years will see a whole new sporting world.

Ian Ward
Hampton, Middx. 1981

Conversion Table

1 lb = 0.454 kg
1 cwt = 50.8 kg
1 gal(UK) = 4.546 l
1 gal(US) = 3.785 l
1 cu in. = 16.387 cc
1 mile = 1.609 km
1 mph = 1.609 km/hr
1 lb/sq in. = 0.073 kg/cm²
1 atmos = 1.035 kg/cm²
1 hp = 0.746 kW

Photographic Credits

National Motor Museum, Beaulieu: 15, 21, 25, 27, 30, 36, 38, 39, 41, 44, 45, 58, 62, 63, 70, 72, 73, 75, 78–83, 89, 90, 92, 98, 103–105, 110, 118, 126, 129, 143, 155.

This 1908 Benz Grand Prix car is a fine example of the thinking of the early 1900s, with a massive 12.5-litre, four-cylinder engine crammed into a small chassis.

A RACING HERITAGE

Dr Porsche's final design for Austro-Daimler was the superb little ADM. This is the 1926 sports version, powered by a 3-litre engine.

It can equally be argued that the road-going sports car was a by-product of competition and that competition itself bred the sports car. As we have seen in the introduction, the sports car has never been universally accepted as a single animal, so both arguments have their merits. It is certainly true that motorised competitions began to spring up even while the automobile was still only finding its wheels, so to speak, and manufacturers and owners forced their primitive machinery into service which was really above and beyond the call of duty.

It is generally recognised that the first organised competition was a trip from Paris to Rouen set up in 1894 by the editor of the French magazine *Le Petit Journal*. However, this event was not a test of speed; the idea was simply to prove the reliability – or otherwise – of the various cars. Nevertheless, the seed was sown and manufacturers such as Comte de Dion began to press for a proper race over a more testing distance, still on the open roads of France. *Le Petit Journal* forbade its editor to take part in the organisation of such an event lest disaster should overtake it resulting in a major set-back for the magazine. Undeterred, Comte de Dion formed a committee to organise a race over the 700 miles from Paris to Bordeaux and back, to take place in the following year, 1895.

There are two basic reasons for the birth of motor sport. The first is man's natural competitive spirit: given any possible test of skill, endeavour or endurance, man will quickly organise competitions with his fellows. This is the essence of all sport; there is an element of simple enjoyment, but the overriding factor is the desire to win. Take away the opposition and most of the fun has gone. The second reason is that it did manufacturers no end of good to prove to the world that their wares were capable not only of travelling long distances reliably, but of getting there more quickly than any other vehicle. Of course, this could backfire if they were soundly beaten or were ignominiously towed home by horses, but it has to be remembered that in those pioneering days most people still regarded the 'horseless carriage' with a great deal of suspicion and many were convinced that four legs would win through in the end.

Most of the early competition took place in France, and there was a very good reason for this. While it was the Germans, in the form of Otto, Benz and Daimler, who had led the way in the development of the internal combustion engine, it was in France that the first flush of small companies building examples of the motor car arose. Moreover, in Britain, which was later to be the home of so many of the great sporting marques, the Government was positively terrified of these infernal machines and was making every effort to legislate them off the roads. The steamers of the earlier part of the century had started the rot, and it was not until 1896 that the Red Flag Act was repealed and the speed limit was raised from 4 mph on the open road and 2 mph in towns to a staggering 12 mph.

So this brings us back to Paris in 1895, with forty-six eager contenders for the outing to Bordeaux. De Dion and his committee had been very cautious in formulating the regulations for the contest, and they stipulated that all cars entered should have a minimum of four seats. This, they hoped, would keep speeds relatively low. As it turned out, the entry was made up of twenty-three petrol cars, thirteen driven by steam and two by electricity; the other eight were motor bicycles or tricycles, of which few, if any, would have had four seats. First across the finishing line was a two-seat Panhard driven by Emile Levassor, who had driven the whole of the distance himself, taking over 48 hours and stopping only long enough to fill the tank. However, his efforts went unrewarded in terms of prizes, his car being disqualified because of its lack of accommodation. The same applied to the second-placed Peugeot, which came home 6½ hours later, and so the official prize went to another Peugeot, in third place on the road. Levassor was by no means down-hearted, however, he knew the rules when he set out and his sole aim was to prove that he and his car could beat all comers.

The success of the two-seat petrol-engined machines gave a clue to things to come. It was fairly obvious that light weight was essential for consistent racing success and it was not long before competition cars had so many holes drilled in their chassis that one wondered whether they had been left to the mercies of a team of mice. Coupled with this, the engines began to take on

Famous boxer Jack Johnson at the wheel of one of Austin's 100 hp racers, unsuccessfully campaigned in the 1908 French Grand Prix.

mammoth proportions. Although this first race was very much a gathering of fairly standard road-going cars, rather than a parade of the purpose-built monsters soon to come, it was the more beefy or more nimble of the standard machines which took the honours, so this was perhaps the earliest example of sports cars breeding racers.

Emile Levassor's Panhard was equipped with only a 1.2-litre, 4 hp engine and yet it offered a maximum speed of nearly 20 mph. However, this sort of performance did not satisfy the 'sports-men' for long; despite the primitive state of most of the French roads of the period, the racers gave not a second thought to the dangers of increasingly high speeds. The Paris–Bordeaux event was a great success and it led to a whole series of road races starting – and sometimes finishing – in Paris: Paris–Marseilles–Paris 1896; Paris–Dieppe and Paris–Trouville 1897; Paris–Bordeaux 1898; a plethora of events in 1899, the stars being Paris–Ostend, Paris–Boulogne and

the 1400-mile Tour de France, starting and finishing in Paris; Paris–Toulouse–Paris 1900; Paris–Berlin 1901; Paris–Vienna 1902. The last of these famous road trials was organised in 1903 and was to be run over a course from Paris to Madrid. However, eager spectators crowded the roads and one tragedy after another befell both the crowds and the drivers, so that the Government called a halt to the event at Bordeaux, banning road racing there and then.

By then, the demise of such events came as no surprise to anyone; not only was it almost impossible to control the crowds over such enormous distances, but the cars, while still remaining extraordinarily crude in the chassis department, were reaching speeds of 100 mph or more. Most of the later Paris racers were purpose-built for the road and bore less and less resemblance to their road-going counterparts. What had started off as stripped tourers became very specialised; until 1902 there were no restrictions regarding engine size or vehicle weight, so the constructors used the lightest possible frames (which in those days often meant the weakest) coupled with engines which would have been more at home in battleships. There were two makes whose cars achieved considerable racing success in those early days, Panhard and Mors; surprisingly, though, neither of these was later to be noted for sports cars.

The main reason for the trend towards ever-larger power units was that the average manufacturer did not have the knowledge to build an engine which would run reliably at either high piston speeds or high crankshaft speeds (1000 ft/min and 1500 rpm were quite good going). The need for secondary engine balancing did not occur to the likes of Panhard, and in any case, the extraordinarily long strokes brought about by eventual restrictions on bore size meant that crankshaft speeds of more than about 2500 rpm, with the then-current cast-iron pistons, brought a real danger of sending the pistons through the cylinder heads. All this meant that the only way this type of manufacturer knew of coaxing more power out of his engines was to increase the capacity. This in turn brought possible speeds down and formed something of a vicious circle. Four-cylinder power units with capacities of 10, 11 and 12 litres were quite common in the early 1900s, with what were then remarkable power outputs of 100 bhp or so. However, they were not always successful in competition. The massive size of these units combined with the flimsiness of the frames in which they were usually mounted was a perfect recipe for disaster. From the point of view of handling, these monsters had great difficulty negotiating anything tighter than a slight bend at speed. On a 'good' road, they would beat a small car easily, but road races were mostly held over a mixture of road types, so the power advantage was drastically reduced. This was first demonstrated in 1902, when Marcel Renault won the light car class and finished second overall in the Paris–Vienna race, driving his own 16 hp car.

This machine's 3.8-litre engine seemed tiny compared with the gigantic 13.7-litre 'lump' of Henry Farman's winning 70 hp Peugeot.

The writing was already on the wall for these leviathans, but the simple answer for the constructors of such beasts was to alter the routes of the marathon events to suit their progeny. It did not occur to them that they were going the wrong way in terms of development. Nevertheless, salt was rubbed into the wound the following year when Louis Renault took a moral victory in the shortened Paris–Madrid race, after his brother, Marcel, had been killed in a similar car.

With the end of the great road races in 1903, it was largely left to the Gordon Bennett series to keep international motor sport alive until the advent of the first Grand Prix in 1906. James Gordon Bennett, a newspaper proprietor, had founded the series which carried his name in 1900, but it was never a great success. Various venues were used, all of them roads closed to the public, and the event was perhaps most noteworthy for the fact that it saw the first use of team colours.

In 1906, the Automobile Club de France, which was based on Compte de Dion's original committee, organised the first Grand Prix, around a triangular circuit based on Le Mans. In an effort to keep speeds down to a 'reasonable' level, the organisers instituted a maximum weight limit of 1007 kg. As it turned out, however, all that happened was that the constructors made their cars' chassis ever lighter and more flimsy in order that they might fit correspondingly bigger engines. For this event, Panhard came up with an engine of 18 litres, but once again it was the comparative baby from Renault, at only 13 litres, which took the main prize.

These cars were so immense and so impractical in terms of highway use that there would seem to have been little use for them in tourer form. However, many of the racers of the day were, in fact, rebodied – or perhaps more correctly bodied – for road use. Mors, for example, achieved considerable success in these early events and the 60 hp racer which Henri Fournier had driven to victory in the 1901 Paris–Berlin race was soon fitted with a four-seat body and driven on the ordinary roads. This was a one-off, but when

Austin's team of Grand Prix cars failed to achieve any success at the French Grand Prix of 1908, they were converted to fast-tourer specifications, which marked the beginning of a line of Austin sports cars. The racers had themselves been based on the chassis of 60 hp tourers, with engines bored out to 9677cc and their lack of achievement was due, more than anything else, to their relatively small size. Their power output was respectable enough, at 170 bhp, but they simply could not keep up with the French and German giants.

The pioneers of British motor racing were undoubtedly the old-established company of Napier. Since the 1820s the company had been in business doing very varied general engineering work, but in 1899 an expatriot Australian called Selwyn Francis Edge brought Napier into the motoring business. Edge purchased a 6 hp Panhard (which had finished second in the Paris–Marseilles–Paris of 1896), but he was not particularly happy with the standard item. A mutual friend suggested that Montague Napier's company would be the one to carry out the modifications which he required, such as fitting wheel, instead of tiller, steering and improving the engine lubrication system. At the time, Napier had had no experience of the fledgling motor industry, but as an engineer he was quick to decide that he could easily improve on the Panhard's engine. He asked Edge what he thought and Edge was delighted to give him the go-ahead to build his own unit for the car. The resulting 8 hp vertical twin, with electric ignition, as opposed to the then-common hot-tube variety, impressed Edge, who was by then installed in his own motor agency in London. Edge then encouraged Napier to make replicas of the engine and install them in a chassis based on that of the Panhard, guaranteeing to sell all that Napier could turn out. It was also Edge who took the company into competition, entering a car in the 1000-miles Trial organised by Britain's Automobile Club in 1900. This was very much a road event, but the Napier won its class and gained a considerable amount of publicity, which boosted sales usefully. After an unsuccessful foray on the Paris–Toulouse–Paris race of the same year, with the soon-to-be-famous Charles Rolls in the mechanic's seat of a four-cylinder, 16 hp car,

Napier followed the trend and built himself a monster. This beast had a 17-litre, four-cylinder engine producing just over 100 bhp at a princely 800 rpm and was actually offered to the public as a catalogued item, although very much a racing car.

Several other of Napier's early competition models were either offered for sale or were subsequently fitted with touring bodies, including the six-cylinder 60 hp and the 1908 Tourist Trophy winner, which was a four-cylinder machine entered as a Hutton because the company was at that time trying to push its six-cylinder models. Although Napier did not invent the six-cylinder engine, the company was responsible for popularising it, after its earlier use by companies such as Spyker. Edge reckoned that by the end of 1906, due to Napier's concentration on units of the type, there were over 140 makes of car with six-cylinder engines.

If few of the early true racers were really suitable for road conversion, there were plenty of ideas first tried out in racing which subsequently found their way on to road-going cars. Indeed, this was just the beginning of what, for many manufacturers, either of components or of complete cars, has since become the *raison d'être* of motor sport. For instance, Mors, on their Paris–Vienna machine of 1902, made the first real effort to keep the movement of the wheels in check on the rough roads of the time by using suspension dampers. In fact these were not just dampers, they were hydraulic dampers which did not to find their way into general use until thirty years later. The first water-cooled cars were equipped with radiators of massive copper tubes in order to keep the engine temperature under control. This system was not very efficient, and it was the Canstatt Daimler 24 hp racer of 1899 which gave the world its first glimpse of the honeycomb radiator – the type commonly used today. The same car exhibited probably the first gate gearchange.

It was competition work which brought about many of Panhard's innovations during that marque's heyday. Almost from the start the company used the now-classic layout of front engine and rear-wheel drive which it had pioneered, but the cars quickly began to sprout an array of modern niceties, such as pneumatic

tyres, aluminium gearbox casings, float carburettors and separate forged-steel cylinder
barrels bolted to the top of the crankcase.
Strangely, however, after Panhard's domination
of the racing scene until the turn of the century, it
was somewhat eclipsed and never really regained
its innovative stature.

Development of racing cars in the 1900s was
taking them so far away from sensible road cars
that the French developed their voiturette racing
class for cars of small engine size and fairly light
weight. This class had been started in the 1890s
by Bollée, when all engines were small. A series of
events was started in 1905, sponsored by the
magazine *l'Auto* and known as the Coupe de
l'Auto, but for some strange reason the method of
restricting engine size, after an initial, straightforward, 1-litre restriction, was to stipulate a
maximum bore, which varied according to the
number of cylinders. Consequently, some un-
scrupulous manufacturers simply produced engines with massive stroke dimensions, such as the
two-cylinder Lion-Peugeot of 1910, which had
an 80 mm bore but a 280 mm stroke. On the
whole, however, the class served its desired
purpose and produced some fine practical cars.
Sizaire-Naudin produced its first car for the road
in 1905, but company fortunes flagged until it
demonstrated its wares 'in anger', entering a car
in the 1906 Coupe de *l'Auto* round. In most
respects the Sizaire, with its 918cc, single-
cylinder power unit was primitive, but it was
noteworthy for its pioneering use of independent
front suspension, this having sliding pillars with
a transverse leaf spring (Morgans still use sliding
pillars today). This was obviously effective, for
the car won convincingly, driven by Georges
Sizaire, and the marque went on to achieve many
more successes.

Another voiturette which was significant in the
development of the road-going sports car was the
delightful little Isotta-Fraschini of 1908. This
stood head-and-shoulders above its opposition,
in terms of design, by having a remarkably

*This 1908 Napier Tourist Trophy winner was
entered as a Hutton because it had a four-cylinder
engine, whereas the company was trying to promote
its six-cylinder range.*

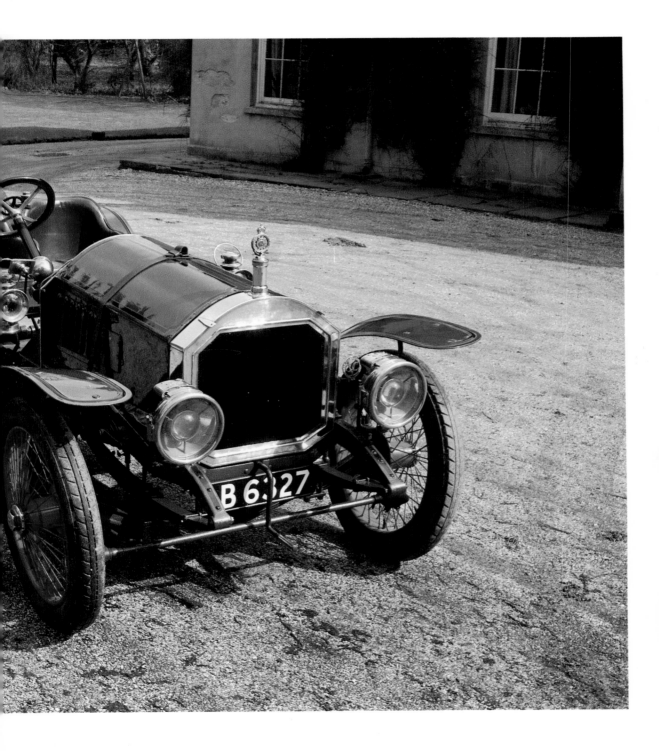

advanced monobloc four-cylinder engine of only 1208cc which could spin happily up to 3500 rpm – an almost unheard of figure for the time. The power unit was also a departure for the company, whose other products at the time all made do with more primitive side-valve units, in that it not only had mechanically operated overhead valves, but it was equipped with an overhead camshaft to open them. Fine as this car was, it did not fare well against the crude and coarse opposition, but it did find its way into production, albeit with its engine enlarged to 1327cc and albeit for only a couple of years, as the 10 hp. In road trim, the Isotta was equipped with a four-speed gearbox, with an overdrive top gear ratio to give relaxed 'high-speed' cruising. The sewing machine precision of the little engine has led a number of historians to suggest that the maestro Ettore Bugatti took a hand in its design – especially as both Isotta and the great man had been associated through Lorraine-Dietrich – but Isotta's gifted young designer, Giustino Cattaneo, claimed the unit as his own creation and it seems likely that Bugatti made careful studies of it when planning his own first baby.

It was voiturette racing which finally brought about the dethronement of the racing mammoths, although this only happened over a long period. Eventually participants and spectators alike were convinced that there were better routes to higher performance than more 'cubic inches'. The Isotta marked the thin end of a wedge of sophistication which began to creep into performance car design. This is not to say that the large engines did not continue to exist and be developed. Indeed, Isotta themselves introduced their production KM in 1909, with a 10.5-litre engine, but this four-cylinder unit was equipped with a single overhead camshaft operating no less than four valves in each cylinder. Strangely the KM was also noteworthy because it introduced brakes on all four wheels some five years *before* such a system first appeared on the race tracks.

The giants may have seen their day, but there was one remarkable racing machine which cannot go unmentioned in a book of this type and that was the 200 hp Benz, better known as the '*Blitzen*'. This first appeared in 1909 and achieved considerable success in competition and record-breaking, particularly in the United States. In 1912 a touring version of the car was catalogued and with its gargantuan 21,504cc, four-cylinder, overhead-valve power unit, it became the largest car ever to be offered for sale, either before or since.

Although the idea of the Coupe de *l'Auto* was to encourage the development of small, light cars, they were not all midgets like the Isotta 10 hp. In 1909 the Spanish Hispano-Suiza marque first appeared in the voiturette field. Swiss designer Marc Birkigt had felt it a matter of honour to design a team of cars to contest voiturette races when King Alfonso XIII, already a patron of the marque, presented a cup for such an event to be held at Sitges, near Barcelona. The cars were built with four-cylinder, 1852cc, side-valve engines (opened by two block-mounted camshafts, one each side of the monobloc cylinders), and one of the team of three led the field until its clutch broke. For 1910, regulation changes allowed bigger engines, but the team still could not take victory in the Catalan Cup, as the Spanish race was known. However, a further enlargement, to 2646cc, for the Coupe de *l'Auto* of that year finally brought the victory which was richly deserved.

This was the first four-cylinder winner of the Coupe and the company decided to turn it into a road car. The inordinately long stroke was shortened and the bore enlarged to give a capacity of 3620cc, but the chassis and general mechanical layout were left largely as on the racers. The most important feature was that the gearbox was mounted in unit with the engine, at a time when it was common for it to be in the centre of the car, driven by a short shaft. The wheels, too, were of advanced design, being of the centre-lock wire type, as opposed to the fixed artillery variety of contemporary machinery. Two chassis lengths were available, as were various bodies, but by far the most common was the open two-seater on the short chassis, which the 64 bhp engine could coax up to an exhilarating 80 mph at a time when speeds of this nature were almost unheard of outside Grand Prix racing.

One of the first customers for the new car in 1910 was the King himself, whose wife bought him one for his birthday. Officially designated the Type 15T, the Hispano soon became known

as the Alfonso and was exported under that name to various countries. Hispano-Suiza opened a factory in France in 1911, so the Alfonso was made in two countries during most of its life, which extended until the outbreak of World War I in France and for another two years in Spain.

Earlier we saw how some sports cars developed from racers and vice versa, but the Sunbeam racers and sportsters of about 1911 were based closely on each other. Around that time, the Coupe de *l'Auto* allowed cars of up to 3 litres, and the Sunbeam racers of 1911, designed for the event, were based on the then-current touring cars, albeit with enlarged engines and improved cylinder heads. As a racing car, this model was not a success, but the new road car of that autumn bore characteristics obviously inherited from it, and it was significant in that a sporting variant was offered for the first time. For the following year, the new racing cars were based on those sports machines and with sleeker bodies and more power than in 1911 they took the first three

A 1912 version of Hispano-Suiza's neat and pretty Alfonso, named after the King of Spain, who was himself one of the first customers for the car.

places in the voiturette class of the Coupe de *l'Auto*. Once again, road-going versions followed, known, as before, as 12/16s, but the competition success of that year was never repeated. However, the sporting car was now a fixture in the Sunbeam list and the Coupe de *l'Auto* 'replicas' were gaining popularity by the outbreak of World War I in 1914.

Although cars such as the Hispano-Suiza and the Sunbeam were real sporting offshoots from motor racing, rather than rebodied 'one-offs', it was long distance road trials such as the Herkomer and Prince Henry events which did most to further the cause of sports motoring. Unlike the Paris races before them, these events were more relevant to everyday motoring in that

they were for road-going cars rather than one-off racers. If anything, these were the predecessors of modern road rallies.

The Herkomer Trial was first held in 1905, over a course from Frankfurt to Innsbruck, and was named after Hubert von Herkomer, who was to paint the winning driver's picture. Strict bodywork regulations and a prize for coachwork meant that most of the entries in that first event were standard tourers, but the following year saw an abandonment of that prize and the consequent 'bending' of the rules to make the cars much more sporting. During the three years that the Herkomer was run, the competitive entries took on a considerably greater sporting air, with lightweight coachwork and the beginnings of streamlining. The Horch 18/22 which took the prize in 1906 was hardly a sports car, although its advanced power unit had overhead inlet valves and ball crankshaft bearings, but a much modified version was the scandal of the first Prince Henry Trial in 1908 and was very much a key figure in sports car development.

Prince Henry of Prussia was the younger brother of Kaiser Wilhelm II, who had himself inaugurated the Kaiserpreis in 1907 for what boiled down to sporting cars of up to 8 litres cylinder displacement (this was won by a special Fiat 'Taunus' model, which was very much a sporting machine). The Prince had been a competitor in the Herkomer Trials and the demise of the event led him to present a trophy for his own touring car event, especially for amateurs. This was planned as a leisurely affair, combining endurance and speed with a certain amount of socialising over a period of a few days.

The regulations stipulated a minimum of four seats in the cars and a maximum cylinder bore size decided by the number of cylinders. However, some of the entrants did not quite follow the spirit of the rules and specially bodied machinery was to be found in the hands of professional drivers. The new Horch 18/22 had light coachwork, admittedly with four seats, of a type which has since become known as the

A 1914 example of Vauxhall's fine Prince Henry; by this time the engine had been enlarged to a full 4 litres and the car could manage 80 mph.

torpedo, with a rounded cross-section and separate compartments for front and rear passengers, entered by climbing over the side. The car's wings were flared to the point of being almost horizontal and wind resistance was reduced by the lack of windscreen or hood. Although it was not realised at the time, the Horch represented the shape of sporting things to come. It was not alone in its style, but it carried the whole theme a little further than did other participants, such as the Opels and the winning Benz of Fritz Erle, the latter being on an altogether larger scale. A 'Prince Henry' car soon came to be thought of as a streamlined, open four-seater, with flared wings, low scuttle and equally low body sides. The event gained considerable popularity because many of the entrants bore an unmistakeable resemblance to the cars which could be bought for road use.

There were two Prince Henry models, catalogued by their makers, which became famous in later years. The first of these was the Austro-Daimler, officially known as the 27/80, which was constructed for the Trial of 1910. Austro-Daimler was the Austrian branch of the German Daimler company, but by this time Paul Daimler had been replaced at its head by Dr Ferdinand Porsche, later to figure so prominently in sports car design. It was Porsche who planned the new machine for the Prince Henry Trial and he decided to use a 5.7-litre, four-cylinder, single-overhead-camshaft engine. There was nothing particularly revolutionary about the power unit, but it managed to rev to nearly 2500 rpm and could produce almost 100 bhp at that speed; quite a step up compared with the car's contemporaries or predecessors. The chassis was a conventional steel pressing and it performed adequately, but Porsche did not believe at that time that shaft drive could cope with 100 bhp, so he took the seemingly retrograde step of using chains for the final drive from the four-speed gearbox.

Retrograde or not, the chains obviously worked, as the Austro-Daimlers took the first three places in the 1910 Trial, Dr Porsche himself driving the winning car. Coachwork of the cars was unusual in that the sides had a sort of positive camber – they sloped outwards at the top – in order to comply with regulations regarding minimum width, while keeping the frontal area down. In this basic style they went into production and between 1910 and the outbreak of war about 200 were made. Later examples had shaft drive and other handsome body styles were used, but the Prince Henry retained its sporting character throughout.

Perhaps better known than the Austro-Daimler was the Prince Henry entry of Vauxhall, which also first appeared in the 1910 Trial. Vauxhall had been responsible for some fairly mundane machinery until they took on and recognised the engineering talents of a young British engineer called Laurence Pomeroy. His real chance came in 1908, when, having committed themselves to entering the Scottish 2000-mile trial of that year, Vauxhall management realised that their chief engineer was off sick. Pomeroy was called in and he designed them a splendid new 20 hp machine which pulverised the opposition. With this win under their belt, Vauxhall began to take competition more seriously and versions of Pomeroy's car were soon taking victories and breaking records at various venues.

For the 1910 Prince Henry Trial, Pomeroy set about the modification of his 20, particularly with a view to extracting more power from its 3-litre, four-cylinder engine. He managed to boost power output from 38 to 60 bhp largely by encouraging the unit to run at higher speeds. To make the most of this extra power he gave the car a new sporting body with a sharply pointed radiator together with low scuttle and sides. Although the Austro-Daimlers took the prizes in the event, the Vauxhalls acquitted themselves well and in doing so attracted a considerable amount of attention. The following year saw a production version of the car, by now known as the C-type Prince Henry Vauxhall, on offer to the public, generally with a sleek four-seater sporting body, at a price of £580. This perhaps gave the average motorist his first real taste of sports car motoring, although the term was not to be coined for another decade. The Prince Henry combined more than adequate power with a hitherto unheard of flexibility and nimbleness.

The Vauxhall sold well, but the company did not rest on its laurels. In 1913 they enlarged the engine to 4 litres, with a consequent power boost to 75 bhp, and made the body slightly more comfortable. However, the model was becoming uncompetitive in races and trials, although it was capable of some 80 mph in road-going form. A competition driver called A. Joseph Higginson approached Vauxhall with a view to building him a car to take the record at Shelsley Walsh a few weeks later. Remarkably, Vauxhall and Pomeroy obliged and provided a modified C-type chassis, with its engine bored to 4.5 litres and producing around 100 bhp. The distinctive V-shaped radiator had been replaced by a flat one, but the body was of sleek shape and light aluminium and the car beat the Shelsley record so comprehensively that the new mark stood for fifteen years.

The new car was soon on offer, under the title 30/98, with a sports tourer Velox body as standard. Unfortunately war intervened with only eight production cars built and it was not until 1919 that the new Vauxhall really made its mark. The company guaranteed a maximum speed of 100 mph with the car stripped, which was probably more than enough for the rather basic chassis arrangement. This version achieved considerable racing success, but in 1922 a new

overhead-camshaft power unit, with a reduced capacity of 4224cc but an increased power output of around 115 bhp, was inserted and what had been the E-type became the OE. Shortly afterwards the chassis was improved when front brakes were added and the car continued in production until 1927, with its Prince Henry cousin becoming one of the most famous of all sports cars.

The idea of long distance road trials really caught on with the Prince Henry events; sophistication was at last finding a place in the motor car in the form of four-valve engines, stiff steel chassis and brakes that actually worked. The Austrian Alpine Trial and the Russian Trial took over from the Prince Henry and spawned a new crop of sporting machinery from such companies as Austin, with their 30 and 40 hp

An Amilcar CGS of 1927 competing in the Ilkley, Yorkshire, club trial. Although the 1100cc engine was not especially powerful, the car was light and performed well.

Defiance models of 1912 on, and Austro-Daimler, with a new 2.2-litre sportster – a positive midget for the Austrian company. Even Rolls-Royce found themselves in motor sport with a modified Silver Ghost, known as the Continental, which took a prize in the Alpine Trial of 1913. By all except the company, this model became known as the Alpine Eagle.

By this time there were all kinds of motor sport events around the world and most were responsible for the development of at least one type of sporting road car. For instance, in Italy the Targa Florio quickly brought on the development of the 4-litre Alfa (before Romeo was involved) in 1911, the company only having been founded in that year. However, war intervened in 1914 and both sport and car development were just about brought to a halt for four years. With the return of peace, most of the pre-war names reappeared, often with revised versions of their earlier cars, but sometimes with completely new machinery.

Austro-Daimler had a great tradition to uphold and Dr Porsche excelled with his final design for the company before moving to Mercédès. The ADM, available with a number of different body styles for road use, was a great success in events such as the Tourist Trophy, initially being powered by a 2.5-litre, twin-overhead-camshaft, six-cylinder engine based on that of Porsche's delightful little Sascha racer. The first true sports bodies were seen on the ADMII of 1925, but in the following year a full 3-litre unit was dropped into the ADMIII to give a possible 100 mph with its 100 bhp.

A new company to rise out of the ashes of the war was the French Amilcar concern, whose first car, the CC was seen in 1920. This was by no means an advanced design, but the company was already showing a sporting bias, most bodies being two-seaters. As the model developed, variants of it were campaigned on the race tracks and the result of this was the beautiful CGS and CGSs models (the latter had the extra 's' for *surbaissé*, due to its lowered line), which appeared in 1924 and 1926 respectively. The engine was an 1100cc four, with straightforward side valves, and was nothing special. However, the Amilcar was light and 35 bhp was enough to give the machine, in Ss form, a top speed of 75 mph. Like many other manufacturers, Amilcar suffered greatly in the Depression, sports cars losing their appeal during those dark days, but they nevertheless built nearly 5000 CGS and CGSs models during their life.

Front-wheel drive was not unknown when the British Alvis company started experiments in racing with it, with a sprint special in 1925. The success of this encouraged the company to build a new racing car for the 1926 Grand Prix formula, again with front-wheel drive and with a new 110 bhp supercharged straight-eight. Success did not come in that year, but the power output was raised to 125 bhp for 1927 by the substitution of twin-overhead camshafts and overhead valves for the strange horizontal valves previously used. Reliability let the machine down, but the lessons learnt were put to good use when a four-cylinder road-going sports car was announced in 1928. Known as the FA, this had a 1.5-litre, single-overhead-camshaft engine producing about 50 bhp in unsupercharged form (a supercharger was an option). The gearbox and final drive were mounted in front of the engine and drove the front wheels through open, double-jointed drive shafts. Suspension was independent all round and brakes were fitted to all four wheels, although, strangely, dampers were a long time coming. The sophistication of the car made it expensive, so few were sold between 1928 and the model's demise in 1931, by which time it had been developed into the FE. However, the model brought the company a great deal of prestige and some competition success, with a top speed, in standard trim, of around 85 mph.

The 1920s saw the upper echelons of motor racing moving away from any similarities to everyday motoring, so that there were ever fewer road cars which could genuinely be thought of as racing replicas. There were still plenty of sports cars based on touring car racers, such as the Cottin-Desgouttes 3-litre model known as the Grand Prix and based on the 1924 Touring Car Grand Prix entry, but the regulations for these events aimed to preclude true racing cars. The knowledge gained during the previous years, and particularly in wartime aero-engine development, had led to the utmost being gained from every cubic centimetre of engine capacity. This in turn meant that racing engines were becoming

steadily less tractable.

One particular exception to this rule was provided by the Italian-born engineering genius Ettore Bugatti. He was designing cars for other companies in the early part of the century, but built the first car to bear his own name in 1910, at his base in Molsheim, which at that time was in Germany although taken over by France after the war. This car, the Type 13, has its own place later in the book, but it is the inception of *Le Patron*'s first production straight-eight, a 2-litre unit, that heightens our interest here. This was first fitted to a prototype called the Type 28, but it did not go into production until the Type 30 was announced in 1922. This was not one of the great Bugattis, for it was noisy and had mediocre brakes, but it did pave the way for one of the most famous sports/racing cars of all time – the Type 35. As is the case with many other manufacturers, there is something of a chicken-and-egg situation with Bugattis and racing; certainly many of the models were raced, but it is not always clear

The Bugatti Type 35 was one of the most famous racers of all time, but much more than this it was equally happy on the road and it is a road-going version of 1926 which is pictured here.

whether they were race-bred tourers or touring racers.

The 30 was certainly raced, and with some success, but it was the Type 35 of 1924 which really took the glory. The 2-litre engine was still used, but its three plain main bearings had been replaced by five of the rolling variety, which reduced vibration and improved reliability. The elegant and simple bodywork has become legend, while touches such as brake drums cast in unit with alloy wheels were examples of why Bugattis came to be treated with such reverence. The 35 was an extremely successful racer and took the World Championship in 1926, albeit by now in supercharged form. Much more than this, though, it was a production racer, which *Le*

Patron insisted could be as happy on urban byroads as on the world's Grand Prix courses. For those who could not stretch to a road-going racer, Bugatti produced four-cylinder, 1.5-litre versions, such as the Type 37 and the Type 40, still with the same jewel-like precision and still with the same superb grace and elegance throughout. The Bugatti company was so prolific throughout its life of nearly forty years that it is impossible to mention all the important models, but needless to say the name features prominently later in this book.

Another name indelibly associated with sporting motoring is that of Aston Martin, the British manufacturer which has had such a chequered career and a variety of proprietors. In the early 1920s, racing was an important sideline for the young company, at that time financed by the famous Count 'Chitty-Chitty-Bang-Bang' Zborowski, but as the 1930s approached, more emphasis was placed on road cars. In 1931, a revised model of the International won a special prize at Le Mans, repeating this success in the following year. This led to an Aston Martin Le Mans replica being catalogued in 1933, with a single-overhead-camshaft, 1.5-litre, four-cylinder engine and two- or four-seater bodywork. This was then further developed to become the Ulster in 1935, with more power and bodywork very reminiscent of the race track models. With its cycle wings and high, side exhaust, the Ulster was capable of over 100 mph and it took many prizes in competition around the world. Sales were always small, but this was one of the few real sports cars on sale in Britain at that time.

In 1931 Aston Martin had a brief marriage to the Frazer Nash concern, founded by Archie Frazer-Nash out of the ashes of the GN cyclecar company. This venture did not prove to be very profitable, but the Frazer Nash company continued in its own right, by this time under the direction of H. J. Aldington. It was the new boss's avowed policy not only that competition improved the breed, but that customer cars

A 1934 Frazer Nash TT Replica. Originally known as the Boulogne II, this model was renamed after running in the TT of 1931.

should be replicas of the racers. The direct result of this policy was one of the most important cars in the company's history. This was originally called the Boulogne II, but after running in the 1931 TT it became the TT Replica, fitted with a 50 bhp, 1.5-litre, four-cylinder, pushrod engine made by Meadows. Frazer Nash cars were most noted for their ingenious transmission system, which seemed particularly crude to many people, yet which proved itself many times over. Basically, a chain-and-sprocket gearbox was employed, fitted at the back axle and open to the elements. There was no differential, but a narrow rear track compensated somewhat for this lack.

At the end of the 1930s the world was once again plunged into war, which effectively halted car development until 1945. Even then, the majority of manufacturers who had survived the war had to make do with updated versions of pre-war models. The influence of motor sport on road cars was perhaps never quite as direct again. The last year of the decade saw the motoring emergence of a man who, in the last twenty years, has been acclaimed as one of the most brilliant designers of modern times – Colin Chapman. Like many other young men at the time, his first efforts at car construction were based on an Austin Seven chassis, which he modified for trials use. The difference between Chapman and the rest, however, was that his ideas soon took him

A 1930 Aston Martin International. This model achieved success both on the road and on the track and, after revised versions had won special prizes at Le Mans, a Le Mans replica was catalogued.

streets ahead of the opposition. This car was Lotus 1 and number 2 was a development of the same theme. However, with his next car he moved into Formula 750 racing and friends started to pester him to build replicas of Lotus 3 and 4. The result of this was that Chapman decided to set up a business selling kits of parts to people who could then add their own standard Ford items where necessary. The car with which he did this was the Lotus 6, a little two-seater with an aluminium skin round a multi-tubular frame. This was fast, handled delightfully, and, most importantly, it began to 'clean up' on the circuits and hill-climbs of Britain.

Enzo Ferrari began to build cars under his own name after the war. Most of them were racers, but road-going versions were offered, with bodywork by such specialists as Pininfarina and Ghia. It was the early 1950s, however, which saw the beginning of a famous line. In 1952 a development car known as the 250 won the Mille Miglia long-distance road race in Italy and by the end of 1953 a road-going variant, known as the 250 Europa was on sale, with a 3-litre V12 under the bonnet, a tubular chassis and a live rear axle. A completely different V12, of the same capacity but from a different designer, was substituted in the following year and the 250 was steadily developed, becoming the 250GT in 1956 and the classic GT Berlinetta from 1959 until the end of production in 1964.

Of course there is little that Ferrari do that is not in some way based on their motor racing experience, but the 250 was one of the first and perhaps best such machines. The same can be said of Maserati in that period; pre-war cars had all been intended for racing, although some had found their way on to the road, but in 1953 the A6GCS 2-litre sports-racing car appeared, with a straight-six, overhead-camshaft engine, itself a Formula Two descendant. Touring versions were offered, with a variety of different coachbuilders' wares, all in the sporting style, but few actually found their way into buyers' hands.

In 1952 Daimler-Benz re-entered motor sport with a sports-racing car called the 300SL. With this, the company took the Le Mans 24-hour race of that year and then went on to astonish the public by announcing that they were going to build replicas of the car for sale. This in fact was a brave move, as the heart of the machine was a multi-tubular spaceframe chassis, which had to be built by hand and was therefore very costly. The engine was a fuel-injected, 3-litre straight-six, producing over 200 bhp. In order to give maximum strength around the doors of this closed coupé, the sills needed to be deep, so gull-wing doors were used, opening upwards and pivoting in the centre of the roof panel. In a straight line, the 300SL was a superb car, with a maximum speed of around 140 mph, but its swing-axle rear suspension made the handling interesting, to say the least. In later cars, this suspension was modified and an open roadster, equipped with conventional doors, was offered from 1957.

Not only was the road-going 300SL descended from a racer, it also sired two other racing cars. One was the W196 Grand Prix car, which although a single-seater owed a great deal to the lessons learnt from the SL, and the other was the 300SLR sports-racer, a version of which Stirling Moss drove to his memorable victory in the 1955 Mille Miglia.

There are plenty of other marques and types of car which have been conceived as a result of competition, but in many cases the link is tenuous or the road-going versions have not been a success. Such machines as the Jaguar E-type and the Ford GT40 most certainly have a racing heritage, but equally they have happier homes in other parts of this book. As a completely new car, the E-type definitely owed a great deal to the C- and D-type Le Mans cars before it, but it was very much a Grand Touring machine. On the other hand the GT40 was definitely a racing car adapted for limited road use, with few concessions to civilisation; it was built for pure performance. Both cars went a long way towards furthering man's quest for speed.

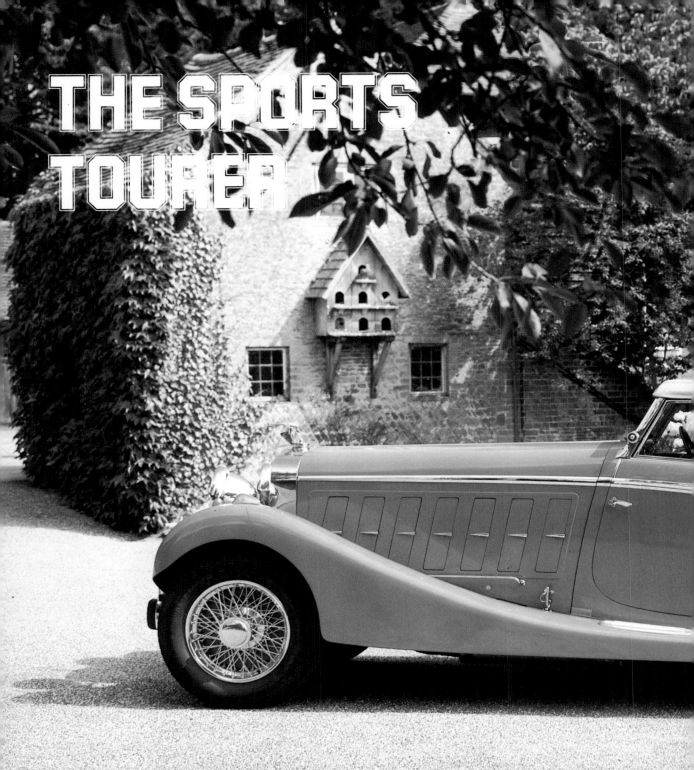

THE SPORTS TOURER

A 1934 Hispano-Suiza type 68bis, whose two-seat convertible cockpit seems lost in the vast expanses of sleek coachwork in front and behind.

Before World War I, sports cars which had been purpose-built or developed from standard road-going vehicles were rare. As we have seen, early road cars were used as bases for the first trials and racing models, which in turn led to the evolution of most of the first road-worthy sports cars. Very few such machines did not have their foundations in competition at that time, although, as is always the case, there were important exceptions to the rule. It is indeed true to say that the vehicle commonly thought of as the first true sports car had no sporting back-ground. This was the 60 hp Mercédès of 1903 and not only was it purpose-built for the road, but it subsequently inherited the role of works racer when the team of 90 hp cars for the Gordon Bennett event of that year was destroyed by fire. However, it would be unfair to classify this father of all sports cars as a tourer. As the racing car grew further and further away from its road-going counterpart after World War I, the sports tourer began to gain more of an identity of its own, without being in any way related to a competition cousin.

It must be remembered, of course, that at this time cars were not built as sports cars or sports tourers, as the terms had yet to be coined. A sports car of pre-World War I days would have been one which was built or modified for competition. As far as road-going machines are concerned, the difference in style between one model and another – or, for that matter, between two examples of the same basic type – was largely due to particular penchants of the numerous coachbuilding concerns. A standard body was almost unheard of, most motor manufacturers offering their wares in chassis form with either a completely free choice of bodywork or at least a wide range of alternatives. Coachbuilding was considered a special craft, not a task to be tackled lightly by mere engineers or mechanics.

So up until the war in 1914 – perhaps until after the war – there was a somewhat vague situation, with very few 'sporting' machines which had no links with competition. As we saw in the first chapter, most road-going sports cars came about as a result of racing experience, but there were certainly some sports cars and sports tourers which were built specifically for the road and subsequently proved in competition.

Mercédès was a company whose name was very prominent in racing at this time, but it built plenty of road cars without any resemblance to the racers of the day. In fact the Mercédès name was linked with, if anything, somewhat staid tourers, although this was probably unfair considering the competition successes and the development of the 1903 60 hp. Having put the Mercédès name on the map with the 60 and with racers such as the 90 hp, Wilhelm Maybach, the company's chief engineer, departed in 1907 and his place was taken by Paul Daimler, son of the company's famous founder. Among Daimler's first designs for the company was a range of tourers with Knight sleeve-valved engines, the most powerful being known as the 16/45PS. As usual, various bodies could be fitted, but despite the somewhat docile nature of the engines, the chassis offered plenty of potential and tourer coachwork was common. By this time, shaft drive had replaced Maybach's favourite chain system and versions of the 16/45 achieved considerable success in Grands Prix.

The reputation for solid reliable machinery was also lent to the Italian Bianchi company at this time. Unlike so many other manufacturers, this concern took very little part in competition, preferring to concentrate its efforts on good road cars. This did not prevent the production of sports tourers, however, and particularly note-worthy was the 42/70 hp model of 1914, which had a four-cylinder, 8-litre, overhead-valve engine in a fairly conventional chassis with chain final drive. In the same category was the Lanchester Sporting 40, also produced in 1914. Lanchester was renowned for highly refined and conservative (if sometimes slightly eccentric) motor cars, but the proprietor, George Lanches-ter, decided that he could reach a wider audience with a sporting inclination. The result was this 5.5-litre, six-cylinder-engined machine, with an epicyclic gearbox and shaft drive. Suspension worked well enough to give the car reasonable handling and the bodywork was very elegant, with separate front and rear cockpits.

The Prince Henry and the Austrian and Russian Trials hastened the development of the sporting car, being more than outright speed trials. However, not every road-going sportster produced by competitors around the time of these events was a direct offshoot of competition policy. For instance, Germany's NSU company had only been in the motor business for a little while when it entered three cars for the 1908 Prince Henry Trial, based on its 10/20 tourers. It also produced a new sporting tourer for production on that base, but the sportster was not a development of the trials machine, it was the result of separate evolution. Known as the 10/30, it had a remarkably small engine, at 2608cc, with a four-speed gearbox and shaft drive. The tourer body was equipped with three doors and four seats and came only in open form, with neither windscreen nor hood.

Austin had turned its Grand Prix cars into tourers in 1908, having failed in competition, but this did not deter the company from entering the Russian Trial in 1910 with a developed 40 hp tourer. This took a prize for a non-stop journey and was soon on offer to the public as the Vitesse, with a 5.8-litre, side-valve engine and open tourer bodywork. A modified engine, with 6.3-litres and more power, was introduced in 1912, with new bodywork to match. This machine, known as the Defiance, was capable of about 85 mph, but it was also much more expensive than the competition, such as the Vauxhall Prince Henry, so it did not sell particularly well. A 30 hp version followed the 40, but before long the names Vitesse and Defiance were transferred to 'sporting' body styles on otherwise standard models. A sporting 20 was built for the 1914 Austrian Trial, but the great promise of this for road use was never exploited, as war intervened.

Several companies previously well known for their sporting activity, such as Mors, began to rely on sporty-looking bodywork rather than improved performance for their sports tourers just before World War I. They made no great claims for their machines, but many motorists were quite happy with a car that simply *looked* unusual. To this end, a number of specialist coachbuilders sprang up; it was their business to 'customise' cars brought to them to make them look both sporty and individual.

World War I interrupted just about all car production and finished off a number of already shaky concerns. It also brought about new motoring requirements. Many manufacturers restarted production in 1919 with slightly modified versions of the machines which they had been selling in 1914, but this was generally a short-lived exercise, new developments coming thick and fast. As we shall see in the next chapter, light cars proliferated in an attempt to take advantage of the new air of optimism. At the outbreak of war, the car had still been something of a novelty, but four years of hard military use had changed that. The sports car and the sports tourer had both begun to find their own identity as racing machinery became more specialised, particularly with the development of new technology during the war. It was mainly in aero-engine design that advances useful to the motor industry were made. New materials, such as light alloys, were developed and cast-iron pistons, for so long the norm, were soon to become a thing of the past. The light materials made higher speeds possible and brought about new heights of engine efficiency. Several aircraft manufacturers themselves turned to the motor industry for their business after the war. Pre-war there had been no real aircraft industry and it was only the exaggerated requirements of the conflict which created enough work to go round. A notable example of this was the Voisin company, which bought the rights to a hitherto unproduced Citroën model and then set about making improvements to it. This was known as the C1 and was equipped with a 4-litre sleeve-valve engine which, in sports form, produced a respectable 90 bhp. The car was available with various types of bodywork, but they were all light, as Gabriel Voisin was dedicated to minimal weights for his cars and introduced such items as tubular connecting rods and magnesium-alloy pistons.

Aero-engines themselves found their way into some machines after the war. This was not usually true of production machinery, but there were a number of one-offs built to make use of some of the mass of war-surplus engines which found their way on to the market. By far the most famous of these was the series of monsters, all called Chitty-Chitty-Bang-Bang, built for Count Zborowski in the early 1920s. The first used a 23-litre Maybach engine in a modified Mercédès chassis and, although originally fitted with a four-seat touring body, was really intended for the track. The second Chitty, built a few months

after the first in 1921, sported a 19-litre Benz aero-engine in the same type of Mercédès chassis, this time equipped with full road-going equipment on its four-seater body. This was still used for competition, but was primarily intended for excitement on the road. The same was true of Chitty III, the last of the series, which was a 'straightforward' conversion of a 28/95 Mercédès chassis, this time the power unit being a 15-litre aeroplane design also from the house of Mercédès. This was very much the Grand Tourer and was taken as baggage tender to Chitty II on perhaps the ultimate Grand Tour to the Sahara Desert. The death of the Count, in the Italian Grand Prix of 1924, brought an end to this somewhat eccentric line, although a fourth design was already in preparation.

During World War I a vast number of allied aircraft had been fitted with engines from the Hispano-Suiza company. It was therefore not surprising that the firm's brilliant designer, Marc Birkigt, should make use of the lessons learnt in his first post-war motor car. This was the H6 and it was the sensation of the 1919 Paris Salon. The 6.5-litre, straight-six engine, with a single overhead camshaft, was derived from one half of a V12 aero-engine design shelved at the end of the war. Light alloy was used extensively, steel liners being screwed into the lightweight block, and the

A 1924 Isotta-Fraschini type 8, with open touring coachwork. This had the world's first straight-eight engine, but it was not considered very good.

seven-bearing crankshaft was carved and machined from a solid block of steel. The chassis seemed conventional enough, but the car's ride was exceptionally smooth yet combined with the most sporting of handling characteristics. At a time when brakes were thought to be unnecessary on the front wheels, Birkigt went one better than a four-wheel system: he added a servo, driven off the gearbox (this system worked so well that Rolls-Royce abandoned their own plans and adopted the Hispano system under licence). On top of all this, the H6 was luxuriously appointed, so that it stood out like a jewel among the pebbles on a beach. In concept, the H6 was not a sporting car, but in execution and performance it deserved the sports tourer description far more than did many purpose-built contemporaries. Success with a short-chassis model in the Coupe Boillot races at Boulogne led eventually to the introduction of the 8-litre H6C Boulogne model, with a 110 mph top speed.

The H6 models remained in the Hispano-Suiza catalogues until 1938, but Birkigt was not one to rest on his laurels. In 1931 came a new

V12-engined machine, the type 68. This 9.4-litre power unit, amazingly with pushrod-operated valves in place of the overhead camshaft (for quieter running), was again based on aero-engine practice, but the car was not particularly advanced in comparison with the H6. However, once again, it was a luxurious machine whose performance put more downright sporting machinery to shame; the 68*bis*, with a 250 bhp 11.4-litre unit had a 100 bhp advantage over its smaller brother. This was undoubtedly one of the greatest of grand tourers.

There were few rivals for the Hispanos in the 1920s, but one which was often compared, albeit unfavourably, was the type 8 Isotta-Fraschini, also announced in 1919. This had the distinction of possessing the world's first production straight-eight engine, in this case a pushrod unit with a capacity of 6 litres. Once again aero-engine knowledge was utilised, but the power output was a mere 80 bhp and the chassis, despite its four-wheel brakes was nothing special. Contemporary critics likened the Isotta to a truck in comparison with the H6 Hispano. Nevertheless, sporting versions of the car were produced, known as the Spinto and Super Spinto, both with 7370cc engines. The Spinto was extra heavy, so the increased power was lost, but the 8ASS of 1926 shed some of that excess and at last gained

Bentley's sports models took a record five victories at Le Mans between 1924 and 1930. The 4½-litre was introduced in 1927 because it was felt that the 3-litre was becoming overstressed and was not fast enough.

some real sporting appeal.

The other motoring sensation of 1919 was caused by a new marque: Bentley. Before World War I, Walter Owen Bentley had been the British concessionaire for the French DFP concern and had devoted some time to improving the performance of this mundane breed. During the war, like many other engineers, he had turned his hand to aero-engine design. In this case, however, his engines were of no direct relevance to what came later, for they were rotary units (in which radial cylinders and the crankcase rotated around a stationary crankshaft, the propeller being fixed to the crankcase). Nevertheless, W.O., as he was known, gained a great knowledge of engine design and of the new lightweight materials and he decided to apply this to a new car built exclusively for the sporting motorist. The result was the 3-litre Bentley, a tourer with a superb single-overhead-camshaft, four-cylinder engine sporting four valves per cylinder and producing 80 bhp. It was not until 1921 that the

car went on sale, but it did so with a guarantee of 80 mph. Various models of the 3-litre were offered over the years, with differing wheelbases and states of tune, but it was competition which brought the company its short-lived commercial success. Between 1924 and 1930 Bentley's took first place at Le Mans on five occasions: twice with the 3-litre, once with the 4½-litre and twice with the Speed Six. Introduced in 1927, the larger 4.5-litre engine not only made the car more competitive, but also gave it more flexibility for the road. Such machines took the first three places at Le Mans in 1928.

Staid touring cars, with six-cylinder engines, had been in production since 1925, but these were not popular. However, Bentley's Speed Six of 1929 combined the 6.5-litre engine with a light sporting chassis and gave a maximum speed of 95 mph. This machine took Le Mans honours in 1929 and 1930 and really marked the end of the line for the company, which was absorbed by Rolls-Royce in 1931. The famous 'Blower Bentleys' – 4½s with Amherst Villiers super-chargers – incredibly were never sanctioned by W.O., who disapproved of the principle. Furthermore, they were never successful at Le Mans. Nevertheless, they did make superb road-

Itala's type 61 of 1924 is seen here with the boat-tailed tourer body typical of the period. As can be seen, the complete car cost £875 in Britain.

going sports tourers.

Itala was a famous pre-war marque which continued to make sporting machines after the Armistice. The type 61 was first seen in 1924 and was a neat sports tourer with a 2-litre, six-cylinder engine. This was capable of pushing the car to a 70 mph maximum speed, but in 1928 twin overhead camshafts replaced the pushrods in the type 65, which was a more sporting car. Sunbeam, too, continued on its sporting way, although competition success began to elude the company. The most notable sports tourer of the 1920s was the twin-cam 3-litre, which was announced in 1924 and raced in stripped form at Le Mans, where it finished a creditable second. The six-cylinder engine produced 90 bhp in unblown form (a supercharger was added in 1929 and boosted power to 140 bhp) and gave the 3-litre a maximum of around 85 mph.

Delage is a famous name in the world of fast touring cars and racers. The 1920s saw the introduction of the D1 in 1924, with a 2-litre,

four-cylinder engine, four-speed gearbox and four-wheel brakes. This was not especially sporting, although it moved well, but it was followed in 1925 by the D1S and then by the D1SS, both of which had improvements to engine and chassis. Performance was not electrifying, with a maximum of around 75 mph, but the cars were smooth, handled reasonably well and, above all, were noted for reliability. The series was discontinued in 1928, but the following year saw the announcement of the new D8, with a 4-litre, pushrod straight-eight and three optional chassis lengths. The 120 bhp power output was enough to give the original D8 a maximum speed of 95 mph, but the model was steadily developed until 1939, when the 4.7-litre D8 120 was producing 140 bhp.

In 1935, Delage was taken over by another French manufacturer, Delahaye, which had hitherto produced some mundane vehicles. The most important result of this was the Delahaye type 135, a 3.2-litre sports tourer with a pushrod straight-six producing 130 bhp. This was used as a basis for a successful competition model and was in production right up until 1950, albeit with sundry modifications. A wide range of bodywork was available, but it is as a fast tourer that the

A works Delahaye 135 of 1936 seen competing at Brooklands in the hands of Arthur Dobson in 1939. DUV 870 was originally campaigned by Rob Walker for the 'works'.

model is remembered.

Italy is a country best known for its opera, its wine and its sports cars. Although most of the Italian cars fall into the category covered in the next chapter, Lancia is a marque which has produced a wealth of sports tourers and saloons since World War I. In 1923 Lancia introduced the Lambda, a highly advanced touring car with no real sporting pretensions. However, this 2.1-litre machine could manage about 70 mph on its V4 engine's 48 bhp and its handling was as good as that of many sporting pretenders. The car was most remarkable for introducing the idea of an integral body/chassis at a time when separate chassis were still very primitive. What is more, it featured independent front suspension in place of the common solid front axle. It remained in production through eight series until 1931.

Lancia has produced so many fine road-going cars with a sporting flavour that it is difficult to single out the best, but there are one or two, apart

from the Lambda, which cannot escape inclusion. The first of these is the Aprilia which was
announced in 1936. It had astonishing
bodywork: the four-door body was endowed
with a sort of 'beetle' tail, which looked very
strange but which gave the car good aerodynamic
drag characteristics, so much so that the 1352cc
engine, again a V4 (with only an 18-degree angle
between the banks), could carry the Aprilia up to
a maximum speed of 80 mph. This Lancia was
also advanced in having a modern type of unitary
body and swing axle rear suspension.

The Aprilia was dropped in 1949 and the
following year saw the birth of another great
Lancia sports tourer (or more accurately sports
saloon), the Aurelia. In this machine a conventional 2.5-litre V6, mounted at the front,
drove the rear wheels through a rear-mounted
clutch and gearbox. Initially, the capacity was
1750cc, but this was steadily increased to 2.5
litres, giving a power output of 118 bhp.
Bodywork consisted of a two-door coupé by

*A Lancia Aurelia GT of 1954. For the GT
version, Pininfarina's elegant coachwork was
complemented by improved performance.*

Pininfarina, with 2 + 2 seating, and the most
sporting version of the Aurelia – and without
doubt the most classic – was the GT, announced
in 1951.

The Fulvia coupé, with its 1200, 1300 or
1600cc, 13-degree V4 driving the front wheels,
was another fine sporting Lancia, made from
1965 until 1976 and very successful in
competition.

The post-war period saw the emergence of
several important new makes and the con-
solidation of many others which had already been
in business before 1914. Many of these were
turning out light cars of one type or another,
which could be sold cheaply and therefore in
large numbers. Such machines formed the bases
for a number of new sports tourers, which fitted

The Lancia Fulvia was made in various forms for nearly twelve years. Pictured here is the Sport S coupé of 1972, with styling by Zagato.

the same bill in that they appealed to the improverished but enthusiastic motorist. After the general strike in Britain in 1926, this type of machine gained even more popularity, as a larger cross-section of the public began to sample motoring as a means of reaching their place of work.

Although most aficionados would blanch at the suggestion that their beloved vehicles are sports tourers, the most important marque to emerge in this category was perhaps MG. The majority of famous cars from this British company undoubtedly fit better into the next chapter, but the firm's foundations certainly belong here. It was the ubiquitous Morris Cowley which provided the wherewithal for MG No 1, although the name had yet to be coined. Cecil Kimber, who was in charge of the Morris Garages, a subsidiary of William Morris's growing empire, began to fit special lightweight bodies to the Cowley (Morris had already stopped making sports versions of this). These were unofficially known as Kimber

Specials and their popularity encouraged William Morris to sanction the production of further Morris derivatives and eventually to set up the MG Car Company, with Cecil Kimber as its Managing Director. It was the 2.5-litre Morris Six which provided the base for one of the MG company's best early machines, the 18/80. This had a light body, coupled with a specially tuned engine and, in Mark II form introduced in 1930, it was particularly notable for the beginning of an MG deviation away from the use of quite so many standard Morris components. The Speed Model 18/80, with a light-alloy and fabric tourer body, was a fine example of a sports tourer, being able to move four people around quickly and comfortably.

Another famous British marque was Riley,

established before the war but not achieving significance until the 1920s. In 1919 a new but conventional light car emerged from the company, powered by a 1.5-litre side-valve engine, which produced a very respectable 35 bhp. This sort of potential was attractive to sporting enthusiasts, and Riley did not disappoint them. In 1923, two- and four-seat sporting versions of the car were announced and, due to the red-painted wings which appended their light-alloy bodies, were soon dubbed Redwings or Redwingers. This model was very successful, both on the road and in competition, but another new model, introduced in 1926 and called the 'Nine', put it somewhat into the shade. The Nine was equipped with a brand new 1100cc engine producing 32 bhp. The novelty of this unit was that it had twin block-mounted camshafts operating inclined valves in hemispherical combustion chambers through short pushrods. Designed by Hugh Rose this engine and its derivatives became standard Riley ware throughout the rest of the company's independent life. The original sporting versions of the Nine were developed by John G. Parry Thomas and, later, Reid Railton and were known as Brooklands Rileys. However, these were not particularly practical for road use and so the Gamecock was announced in 1932 and joined in the range by the Lynx and the Lincock. There was also a new Nine-based two-seater called the Imp in 1934, which was capable of around 75 mph, and the same chassis was available with a 1.5-litre, six-cylinder version of the engine and known as the MPH. Other sporting Rileys abounded during the 1930s, notably the Sprite, which was fitted with a new 1496cc, four-cylinder power unit and a preselector gearbox.

Unlike Rileys, Wolseleys were themselves related to Morris products; the Hornet began its life as a six-cylinder version of the Morris Minor, but was nothing particularly special apart from the fact that it was about the cheapest 'six' available. In 1932 the company decided to offer a sporting version of the car, known as the Hornet

Versions of Riley's Nine were numerous, but the most famous two-seater was the Imp, introduced in 1934 and capable of 75mph.

Special. This had a tuned version of the 1300cc engine, producing about 45 bhp, and was good for about 70 mph. No standard body was offered, the car being available from the manufacturers only in chassis form. This meant that a great variety of coachwork styles could be had, with two or four seats, some very pretty, some downright disastrous.

There was plenty of innovation in the 1920s, as we have seen, but there were also plenty of sports tourers which simply functioned efficiently without boasting any gimmicks. One such was produced by the Italian OM company and known as the 665 Superba. Based on a solid four-cylinder tourer of 1920, the Superba had a 2-litre, six-cylinder, side-valve engine and was available with saloon, sport or sports tourer coachwork, all from the OM company itself. Staid its design may have been, but tuners managed to coax plenty of power out of the engine and the Superba saw a considerable amount of competition success before the company opted out of the car business in the 1930s.

The 1920s came to a close with the world in the depths of depression. Of course, this brought about the demise of many motor manufacturers around the globe, but it particularly affected those who specialised in sporting machinery. After all, was not a sporting car an indulgence – a luxury which one could easily do without?

One great marque which managed to carry on through the difficult years and which has since gone from strength to strength, is Fiat. After building giant racing cars before World War I, the Italian company 'came to its senses' and began to race small, efficient machines. This efficiency was reflected in its touring products, but sporting tourers consisted of different bodies and very little else. Typical of this was the 501S of 1921, which could manage 60 mph, but was hardly worthy of the S suffix. However, in 1933 Fiat produced one of its most famous machines, designated the 508S or Balilla. This was mechanically very closely based on the saloon 508, but its body was all new and the car handled delightfully. Various body styles were available, but all were either open or closed sportsters or sports tourers. In 1934, the valves were relocated above the pistons of the 1-litre engine and this raised the maximum speed from about 60 to 70 mph.

Mercédès is a name which achieved greatness

The two-seat variant of Riley's Redwing, so named after the colour of its mudguards. Announced in 1923, the Redwing performed well on both road and track.

A two-seater version of the OM 665 Superba, built in 1926. The neat coachwork of this example was by Compton and Jarvis.

early on in motoring history. The year 1926 finally saw the merging of the two great rivals Daimler (who produced Mercédès) and Benz. It was at this point, incidentally, that the marque officially lost the two accents. This distinguished company has produced many sporting variants during its long career and it is particularly difficult with such machines to draw a line between purpose-built sports cars and sporting tourers; after all, most Mercedes sports cars have been very comfortable and practical, but they have also had very good performance. Our solution is to include the true roadsters here, leaving the 300SL in the first chapter and the famous 60 hp still to come.

The company used its aviation experience to develop supercharged engines after World War I and the first successful sporting incarnation of such a unit was in the 36/220S of 1927, designed by Ferdinand Porsche, who had joined the company in 1922. This 180 bhp, six-cylinder machine was the first of the magnificent S-class range so famous today. With the Mercedes

system, the supercharger could only be engaged by pressing the accelerator against a very stiff spring; it was not recommended that this should be sustained for more than 15 seconds. This model could manage nearly 110 mph with a four-seater body, but more was yet to come, in the shape of the 7.1-litre 38/250SS, with 200 bhp available. This was also offered with a short chassis, in which form it was known as the SSK and was hailed as one of the most elegant cars ever to be constructed.

The successor to these fine vintage machines was the 500 series, introduced in 1933 with a 5-litre straight-eight (having the same supercharger arrangement) producing about 150 bhp. Various bodies were offered, but even the saloons could not hide their sporting breeding and expansion of the engine to 5.4 litres simply heightened this impression.

More recently the Mercedes sporting flag has been carried by a series of machines launched in 1963. The first of these was the 230SL, with its 2.3-litre straight-six, and a so-called 2 + 2 body (the hard top version of this had a very distinctive concave roof line). Through the 1960s the engine grew through 2.5 litres to 2.8 with the 280SL, which was itself replaced in 1972 by the 350SL, with a V8. Once again this machine has grown and in 1980 had a capacity of 4.5 litres.

There are many people who would argue that Jaguar is a far more sporting name than Mercedes. The 1930s saw the first whole cars to come from William Lyons, the legendary figure behind the Jaguar marque (his Swallow company had previously built only special bodies). The SS1 appeared in 1931 with a 2-litre, six-cylinder Standard engine and a low, sleek body. Not only was this a fine example of craftsmanship, but like all the cars subsequently produced during (Sir) William Lyons' reign it was produced at an unbelievably low price. In 1936 the Jaguar name appeared for the first time on a saloon called the SS Jaguar; the public was also introduced to the two-seat SS100, but that belongs elsewhere. It would be true to say that just about all Jaguars have had a sporting quality to them, but there are one or two which particularly deserve mention as sports tourers (as opposed to the outright sports cars which we will look at later). The six-cylinder XK engine introduced in 1948 found a home in every Jaguar thereafter and gave very sporting performance. The Mk 1 and Mk 2 saloons in particular were renowned for being graceful yet lively, especially in 3.8-litre form. More recently, the XJS has epitomised the luxury sports machine. Its 5.3-litre V12 can carry its sleek 2 + 2 body up to over 150 mph, with hardly a murmur from outside creeping into the passenger compartment.

The Depression did not deter Captain Noel Macklin from building a sports tourer. In the 1920s, Invicta had built a number of models, but

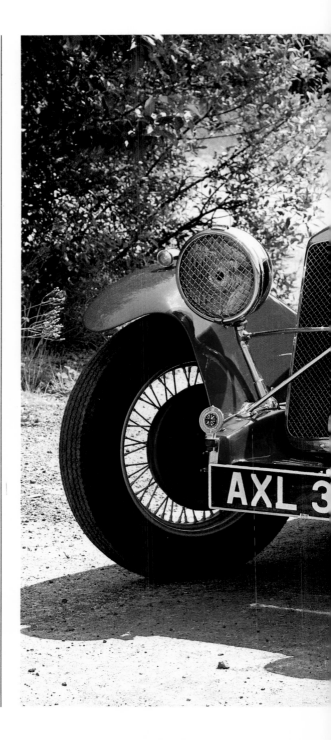

Wolseley's Hornet started out as a six-cylinder Morris Minor, but the Hornet Special had a different chassis and a tuned engine. This is a 1934 two-seater.

The massive Mercedes 38/250SS of 1929 was powered by a supercharged 7.1-litre straight-six. Even in this four-seat tourer form this machine was capable of nearly 120mph.

Invicta's 4.5-litre Model S of 1930 was a fast and handsome machine, but its chassis really was not good enough for its performance and improvements came too late.

in 1930 they announced the 4.5-litre S, with a Meadows six-cylinder engine and extremely expensive tourer coachwork. The S was fast, but it was some years before the chassis and brakes caught up with straight-line performance. By this time it was too late to save the company, and it closed in 1938.

Typical of the 1930s sports tourers was the Lagonda 4.5-litre series, which saw the light of day as the M45 in 1933. Lagonda had been making cars since before World War I and most of them had possessed a sporting air. In its first form, the $4\frac{1}{2}$, with its pushrod Meadows engine, like that of the Invicta, was a little ponderous, but it was soon updated to become the M45 Rapide. Under the direction of W. O. Bentley, whom new owners appointed chief designer in 1935, this turned into the much more refined LG45 shortly after, the Rapide name persisting for the open tourers. W.O. also designed a 4.5-litre V12 which he fitted to a new machine, the LG6 (also available with the Meadows) in 1937. This was the last, and probably the best of the $4\frac{1}{2}$s, World War II intervening in production, the jigs for the engine being destroyed by aerial bombing. Bentley's last design appeared after the war, in the shape of a twin-overhead-camshaft six, which in numerous sizes found homes in a further series of distinguished tourers, culminating in the Rapide of 1961 (by this time David Brown owned the company and the engine is more famous for its Aston Martin use). The Lagonda name has not died, however, for Aston Martin still use it both as part of their company name and as the title for their 5.3-litre, four-seat executive express.

Talbot is a name which has recently come back into the public eye, but, like Lagonda, it was a name in the 1930s which was closely associated with sporting tourers. The most famous of these was the Talbot 90, which arrived in 1930 when a new 2.3-litre engine was dropped into an existing chassis. In tuned form this car achieved considerable sporting success, as had the Lagondas

in the 1930s. Larger-engined 65, 95 and 105 models were then produced, but the company was subsequently taken over by the Rootes Group and the new cars they produced were nothing but disguised Hillmans and Humbers. The one good thing which came of the Rootes takeover was the Sunbeam Alpine of 1953, which was a roadster based on the Sunbeam-Talbot 90, named after the company's successes in the Alpine Rally. This Alpine, however, should not be confused with the rather ordinary confection of the 1960s and a later mundane saloon.

The Talbot name, albeit from the French rather than British company, was also noteworthy in the 1930s for its attachment to a line of sports saloons and coupés known as Talbot-Lagos (after Antony Lago, who had taken over the Sunbeam-Talbot-Darracq concern in 1935).

Triumph is a marque which is indelibly associated with sporting cars, although it has turned out some extremely undistinguished saloons. The first sporting variants, like those of so many contemporaries, were produced in the 1920s, in the shape of the sports Super Seven – based on the 832cc saloon – and later the Gnat. In 1933, however, the Southern Cross was announced, a four-seat sports tourer with a 1.1-litre engine, and this was later updated to become the Gloria Southern Cross, with 1.2, 1.5 or 2-litre engines. Successor to these cars was the Dolomite, which was available with either the 1.2-litre four or the 2-litre six. Saloons were available, but it was the tourers and particularly a roadster of 1938, built at the instigation of Donald Healey (technical director), that were the most popular.

In 1939 war once again halted almost all car production on the European side of the Atlantic and even at the end of the war it was some time before production resumed fully and even longer before many really new models appeared. Unlike the years after the Great War, there was no postwar boom – just a deep despondency created by hardship and rationing. There was certainly very

Overleaf : Lagondas were much improved in the 1930s by the introduction of a $4\frac{1}{2}$-litre V12 engine, designed by W. O. Bentley. This was housed in 1937 in a new tourer, the LG6.

Previous page : this 4.5-litre Talbot-Lago of 1950 was near enough a single-seater, yet it was raced at Le Mans in that year.

little money available to buy the sort of luxury sports tourer which had become popular in the years just before the outbreak of war. What is more, development of the car in general has meant that there has been less and less demand for sports tourers, as opposed to straightforward road-burners or bone-shakers. American regulations for a time were so unpredictable that manufacturers were loath to make convertibles lest they should not be able to sell them in what had become a very lucrative sporting market. However, there have been some milestones along the touring way since the war; some of them we have already seen, but there are one or two more which we must mention.

Although World War II, like its predecessor, produced a vast number of technical innovations for the motor industry – in this case materials, manufacturing techniques and such modern commonplaces as multigrade oils – new manufacturers were few and far between. It was therefore rare to find an aircraft company turning to car manufacture at this time, although this is exactly what the Bristol Aeroplane Company did in 1947, when it announced its elegant 400 sporting coupé. This came about as a result of the company taking over obsolete BMW designs at the end of the war. The engine was basically the 2-litre, six-cylinder unit of the BMW 328, while chassis and body were closely linked to those of the 326 and 327, respectively. This was the start of a long and distinguished line of high-priced but extremely high-quality motor cars, all of which have had sporting connotations, although superficially they have been two-door saloons. The 407 of 1961 saw the first major change, when the old engine was replaced by a Canadian Chrysler V8, which has remained the driving force behind all successive Bristols. One inter-

The popular Triumph Dolomite roadster of 1938 was built at the instigation of Donald Healey. As can be seen it had two permanent seats, with a 'dickey' behind.

esting trademark of most of these tourers is that
the battery and the spare wheel are fitted in the
body panels behind the front wheels.

The BMW engine also found its way into other
homes, most notably that of AC, who employed
Bristol-manufactured units in many of their
post-war cars. The story of the British AC
company goes back to before World War I, but
until the 1950s, the concern was best known for
its series of cars, launched in 1919 and all using
the same basic 2-litre, six-cylinder engine (not
the BMW unit). During its life the engine was
fitted to all types of AC, from two-seat sports cars
to four-seat saloons, and by the time it was finally
discontinued in 1963 its power output had risen
from 35 bhp to 103 bhp. Like Bristol, AC is a
name inextricably linked with sporting cars.
Some, like the Ace and Cobra, belong in the next
chapter, but there were also some fine tourers,
such as the Greyhound of 1960, with a four-seat

*A two-seat version of the Triumph Gloria
Southern Cross built in 1936. This was an
improved edition of the earlier Southern Cross.*

coupé body, the Bristol engine and such niceties
as disc front brakes with coil spring and wishbone
front suspension.

Like so many other motor companies, the one
founded by Richard and Alan Jensen reached
great heights of success before finally tumbling
down in the 1970s. The brothers began their
motor manufacturing careers by building specials on Austin Seven or Standard Nine chassis,

*The first car design to come from the Bristol
Aeroplane Company was the classical 400 of 1947,
which was closely based on obsolete BMW designs.
This is a 1949 example.*

The 328 of 1960 was one of BMW's best and most famous models and its engine was used by both Bristol and AC. Indeed, this 1938 example was equipped with a Bristol cylinder head.

The 'R' version of Jensen's 541 was equipped with a specially modified six-cylinder engine to boost top speed to more than 125mph. It also had all-round disc brakes.

An AC 2-litre Six of 1925. This was one of the early homes of AC's ubiquitous six-cylinder engine, which survived from 1919 until 1963.

and it was not until 1934 that Jensen Motors Ltd came into being. The company's first car was a four-seat tourer called the White Lady, but it marked the first appearance of a characteristic which reappeared in later Jensens – an American V8 engine.

Many of Jensen's cars were straightforward saloons, but in 1953 a fine sports tourer called the 541 appeared, powered by a 4-litre, six-cylinder Austin engine, which gave it a maximum speed of around 115 mph. Over the next few years, this glassfibre-bodied car underwent a series of modifications, one of which was to make it one of the first production four-seaters to be fitted with disc brakes all round. At around this time, Jensen were producing bodies for Austin's A40 sports car, which the brothers had styled, and it was this which led Austin to supply the 4-litre engines.

In 1963 the 541 was replaced by a new CV8, which, although it bore a distinct family resemblance and still used a glassfibre body, was very different under the skin. It had a completely new chassis and was fitted with a 5.9-litre Chrysler V8 engine, which gave it a maximum speed of 130 mph. It was on this car that Jensen first experimented with the Ferguson four-wheel-drive formula, producing a car called the FF in 1965.

By the mid-1960s work on a completely new car, with a body designed by Touring of Milan, was in hand. This was to be the Interceptor which appeared in 1966 with, for the first time, steel bodywork (the bodies being produced by

In 1963 Jensen announced the new CV8, which although it bore a distinct resemblance to the 541 was powered by a 5.9-litre Chrysler V8.

Vignale) and a 6.2-litre Chrysler V8, which propelled it to more than 140 mph. The Interceptor was a great success and once again a four-wheel-drive version was offered. Unfortunately this Jensen in itself was not enough to support the company, which found itself in difficulties when 'bread-and-butter' contracts with other companies began to fall through. The Jensen concern changed hands in 1968 and managed to continue Interceptor production, even producing a beautiful convertible in 1974. However, the small, Lotus-engined Jensen-Healey was not as good as it might have been and it could not save the company.

The exotic Italian makes are renowned for their pure sports breeds, but most of them also make fast tourers, for those that require more seats and perhaps a generally higher level of refinement. After a false start with the Marzal, Lamborghini brought out their Espada, a full four-seater, with front-mounted 4-litre V12, at the end of the 1960s. That company's revered rival, Ferrari, lists one of the most stylish executive expresses ever, in the form of the 400, which offers over 150 mph from its 4.8-litre V12, but which has the accommodation and appointment of a four-seat saloon.

Maserati went one better than either of these,

with their Quattroporte of the early 1970s, which could boast four doors as an accompaniment to its civilised seating. The relative upstart manufacturer, De Tomaso, listed a tourer, in the form of the front-engined Longchamp, and the Italian-sounding Swiss name, Monteverdi, found itself on the long-wheelbase 2+2, the 375L, powered by a 7-litre Chrysler V8.

As we have seen, the sports tourer has become a less popular and less readily identifiable breed, the majority of drivers satisfying their sporting instincts either by fitting 'go-faster' stripes to their cars and buying string-backed gloves, or by specifying tuned versions of standard saloons when placing their orders. In some cases, these machines have been 'breathed on' by outside tuning specialists, as in the case of the original Lotus-prepared Cortina, the series of Fiat-Abarths and Gordini versions of various Simca and Renault saloons. Other manufacturers rely more on their own skills – at least as far as the public is concerned – so that we are offered such delights as Triumph's ingeniously concocted four-valve Dolomite Sprint, Vauxhall's Chevette with a 2300cc engine shoehorned into it and Ford's somewhat more sophisticated but less exciting Escort RS2000. Volkswagen are not being left out of this game either, listing their fuel-injected GTi version of the Golf saloon. The list goes on, but one cannot forget Sir Alec

It was with the CV8 that four-wheel-drive experiments started, but the system was taken more seriously in the reclothed FF of 1966, with steel bodywork by Vignale.

Issigonis's fabulous Mini, of which there have been five Cooper and Cooper S variants, not to mention the slightly more subdued 1275GT.

Turbocharging is an exercise which has come to the fore in recent years as a means of endowing an engine with greater power if such power is required. In other words the driver has control over this, power output – and fuel consumption – varying greatly with the weight of the right foot. The first such machine to be a standard catalogued item, the BMW 2002 Turbo, was somewhat basic, but since then, with machinery such as the Saab 99 and 900 Turbo, turbocharged cars have gained a new sophistication.

A turbocharged engine is also listed by Lotus, for its Turbo Esprit. However, this has not yet found its way into that company's excellent sports tourer of the 1970s and 1980s, the Elite, which combines superb handling and roadholding with enough accommodation for four average people. The 2.2-litre, four-valve, four-cylinder engine does not give electrifying performance, but there is no doubt that this is one car which is keeping alive the notion of the sports tourer.

"A BREED APART

As we have seen, most of the cars with sporting characteristics which were built prior to World War I were from stables noted for their efforts in motorised competition; most of them were spin-offs from racing machines, or the machines themselves. Bearing in mind that no manufacturer was consciously offering a sports car, the term not having been invented, there were only a few companies dealing in cars for enthusiasts and having no interest in competition. Equally, there were few products coming from the racing entrants which were wholly divorced from the beasts of the track or road trial.

As earlier chapters have also shown, there is a very fine dividing line between the early sports tourers and their supposedly more overtly sporting cousins, purpose-built for the enthusiast rather than the family or the chauffeur. However, there are a number of highlights of this pre-war period, some of which certainly led the way for later sports car development.

Daimler was a company whose name was very closely linked with those early days of motor sport (although it was the trademark Mercédès, adopted in 1901, which quickly found its way into lights). Quite fittingly it was a Mercédès which came to be widely regarded as the first road-going sports car, but remarkably this machine, the Mercédès 60 hp of 1903 was very much a touring car rather than a racer. The racer of the period was a 90 hp car and a team of three such vehicles was entered in the Gordon Bennett event which took place in Ireland in 1903. Shortly before the race, however, a fire at the Daimler factory destroyed the three cars, so the company had to resort to the only alternative machine, the 60. Even so, there was no car available for a 'works' entry, although two 60s were already being entered privately. Fortunately an American owner offered to lend his machine to the company for the race, so this was stripped and slightly modified for Camille Jenatzy to drive. In an epic campaign, Jenatzy held off all challenges to win the event outright by

Previous page: Lamborghini's first car was the 3500GT of 1965, with styling by Pininfarina and power from Lamborghini's own 3.5-litre V12.

11 minutes, his relatively diminutive, 9.2-litre, sports car vanquishing the might of René de Knyff's giant 13.7-litre Panhard racer.

The Mercédès 60 was one of the first cars to show that sheer capacity was not an automatic key to success; Jenatzy's win was the first of many for the 60, which soon ousted the 90 from favour. Wilhelm Maybach had already shown the way for the modern car when he designed the first Mercédès in 1901. His 60 hp of two years later took this theme a little further with its pressed-steel chassis (when armoured wood was common), mechanical rather than automatic inlet valves, a gate-change for the gearbox, magneto ignition (with an alternative dynamo system) and an efficient honeycomb radiator at a time when other manufacturers were making do with a few large-bore tubes with gills scattered around on them.

Strangely, although this Mercédès was a sporting trendsetter, the Daimler company subsequently gained a reputation for producing somewhat staid vehicles (particularly with a switch to Knight sleeve-valve engines in 1913).

One manufacturer very much associated with motor sport in the early part of the century was De Dion. We have already seen how the Count himself was a driving force in the organisation of early events, but although the company was very much involved, being the largest independent supplier of engines, it actually built very few complete racing cars. Its only sporting machine of the period was constructed to cash in on the success – albeit in the chassis of others – of its 1250cc single-cylinder engine, particularly in the Coupe de *l'Auto* races. This machine, known as the Type de Course, was very closely based on the standard machines of the day, but it had an attractive two-seat body and could manage a very respectable 50 mph.

The Type de Course appeared in 1909 and it was also in that year that the basis for one of the best pre-war sports cars made its debut. Unlike De Dion, Crossley had very tenuous links with motor sport and its 12/14 (which was actually a 15 hp car) had no sporting pretensions when it was introduced. However, private owners did campaign some examples of the machine at Britain's Shelsley Walsh hill-climb, and Crossley decided to give the Shelsley name to the sporting variant of the car, announced in 1913. Its engine was enlarged from 2.4 to 2.6 litres and was a four-cylinder side-valve unit. With rounded radiator and sleek two-seater bodywork fitted to the car, this engine could push the Shelsley to nearly 70 mph and the chassis offered handling to match. Crossley is much better remembered for its attempt at innovation twenty years later with its version of Sir Dennistoun Burney's weird rear-engined Streamline saloon, but the Shelsley was one of the few sports cars to come from a distinctly non-sporting maker before World War I.

Bugatti is a name indelibly stamped on the world of sports cars and it was in 1910 that the now-legendary Ettore Bugatti announced his first production car, the Type 13. This had been preceded by a fine little 'prototype' built in the cellar of Bugatti's house in Cologne. At the time, 1908–9, he was still under contract to the Deutz company, so his little car was privately called *le Pur-Sang*, which means 'thoroughbred' – a fitting description for just about any of Ettore's motoring creations. In 1909 he found a disused dyeing plant in the Molsheim district of Alsace and set up his new works. Here he constructed his new Type 13, based on the lessons learnt and styles set by his Type 10 (*le Pur-Sang*). The water-cooled, 1327cc, four-cylinder engine established a pattern for many Bugattis to come, with a single overhead camshaft operating the valves through curved sliding tappets. Two- or four-seater bodywork could be had, but in the former style the machine weighed only 11 cwt, so the 30 bhp engine could propel it at the then astonishing speed for such a small machine of 60 mph. The Type 13 was a gem and it captured the motorist's imagination, bringing proper engineering and exceptional road manners to the small car field. Types 15 and 17 were slightly larger versions of the 13, but it was the post-war Brescia models, named after their success in the Brescia race of 1921, which became the most famous. By this time, the engine had grown to 1496cc, and with four valves instead of two per cylinder, the Brescia was capable of 90 mph.

It is well known that light cars such as the Bugatti began to gain popularity in the years after World War I, but this was preceded by a craze for a wave of mostly primitive machines known as cyclecars. This new fashion came about partly due to high taxation and partly due to the impecunious motor cyclist's desire for more wheels and (possibly) greater comfort. Few examples could really be described as sporting, except for the fact that most of them were so crude that their drivers required at least a sporting spirit. Many cyclecars were thoroughly nasty devices, but they were all cheap and there were one or two notable examples.

The Bédélia was an extremely crude machine, with a front-mounted vee-twin engine, final drive by enormous belts and a long, spindly body with tandem seating (the driver at the rear). Needless to say this French machine was very light and so was capable of 60 mph in sports form, a speed which must have been exciting to say the least, with a centre-pivot steering system seemingly inherited from a child's box cart. Notwithstanding the crudity and the apparent danger of operation, the Bédélia was popular and even survived into the 1920s; what is more, it achieved considerable success in the Cyclecar Grands Prix of the time.

This French contraption first appeared in 1910, which was also the first year of the British GN, an altogether more practical cyclecar. Like the Bédélia, the GN, named after its constructors, H. R. Godfrey and Archie Frazer-Nash, used a front-mounted vee-twin – in this case a 1-litre JAP unit (later replaced by an engine of the partners' own construction). Also like the Bédélia, the GN was fitted with twin-belt final drive. However, the bodywork was a little more conventional, with side-by-side seating, and the steering mechanism, although novel in operation, was fairly conventional at heart. Sporting variants were plentiful and were successful on the circuits, creating considerable interest from abroad. During the years just prior to the war the cyclecar movement really caught on and new manufacturers seemed to spring up every day in Britain and France. However, very few such concerns survived the war, as did Bédélia and GN, the latter's founders subsequently going on to even greater things with HRG and Frazer Nash.

Anyone thinking of traditional sports cars in the 1980s would surely be hard-pressed not to put Morgan at the top of the list, the company's

1980 models bearing all the hallmarks of 1930s thoroughbreds. However, Morgan's story goes back much further than that, to the cyclecar boom. H. F. S. Morgan announced his first three-wheeler (this type of machine had tax advantages on top of those of the light car) in 1910, but it was success in the Cyclecar Grand Prix at Amiens in 1913 which prompted the company to announce a sporting variant in the following year. This was known as the Grand Prix and was powered by an 1100cc JAP engine, driving the rear wheel through a two-speed gearbox and chains. Like GN and Bédélia, Morgan survived the war; unlike them, though, Morgan went from strength to strength, a fourth wheel finally appearing in 1935. After the war, the Grand Prix model was replaced by the more famous Aero, which was fitted with various types of vee-twin, and this eventually gave way to the more sophisticated Super Sports model of 1929, with a top speed of more than 80 mph.

Although the more professional cyclecar builders outlasted World War I, the boom of the immediate post-war period spelt the end for the vast majority. No longer did cheap motoring mean a spartan existence: a new breed of low-cost light cars made civilisation obtainable for the impecunious motorist.

Perhaps the most famous machine in this class was the Austin Seven, which was introduced in 1922 with a tiny 750cc, side-valve, four-cylinder engine and reasonable accommodation for four people. Variants of the baby Austin were legion, either in terms of body type or of changes made during the machine's seventeen-year life, and there were plenty of sporting varieties, the first of which appeared in 1924. This was a sports car in styling only, but racing driver E. C. Gordon England devised a specially tuned version of the Seven based on his own racing models and called it the Brooklands. This was guaranteed to manage 75 mph, although such a speed would probably have required a brave driver at that time. By 1928, the Seven had been improved

Morgan stayed faithful to the three-wheel principle, producing a long-succession of vee-twin-powered machines. This is a JAP-engined variant of 1930.

considerably in mechanical terms and a Sports
Seven was now a catalogued item with the option
of a supercharger. The most noteworthy sporting
Seven, however, was the Ulster model of 1929, so
named after its good performances in the Ulster
TT, and based very closely on the Sports.

To a large extent the Austin was in a class of its
own during its sporting life, but one serious
British rival came in the shape of the MG
Midget, which appeared for the first time in
1928. Although Morris Garages boss Cecil
Kimber had already produced several Morris-
based sports cars, this was the first of a long series
of machines which to many enthusiasts are the
only real sports cars. The original Midget was
based on the Morris Minor, which was equipped
with an 847cc, single-overhead-camshaft, four-
cylinder engine. The chassis was modified, the
suspension improved, a smart two-seater body
added and the new MG was thus capable of
65mph. Morris themselves were offering a sports
version of the Cowley at this time, but the MG
represented much better value for money.
Kimber was not one to rest on his laurels and this

*The Austin Seven is surely one of the most famous
small cars of all time and over the years sporting
versions have abounded. The best known of these
was the Ulster of 1929.*

M-type Midget was superseded in 1932 by a new
J-type, incorporating lessons learnt from the
construction of record-breaking cars. All the
Midgets were sports cars, even though some were
available with four-seat bodies, and the model
went from strength to strength, both in production and in competition, for which special
versions were produced. The major change came
in 1936, when a new 1292cc pushrod engine
replaced the old overhead-camshaft unit for the
TA, which also had greater comfort and better
brakes.

The most famous of all the Midget species was
undoubtedly the TC, which ousted the very
short-lived TB (which had another new engine, a
1250) in 1945. About 10,000 of these were
produced before the all-new TD appeared in
1949. For most MG enthusiasts, the Midget

MG's Midget series survived for more than 25 years. By far the best-loved Midget of all was the TC, produced for four years immediately after World War II.

series then went downhill, the chassis of the TD being from the Y-type saloon. However, the TD reached nearly 30,000 buyers in its four-year life, which is more than could be said for the final version, the TF. This lower, sleeker car simply did not meet with approval and it was replaced by the very different MGA in 1955. This handsome coupé (open or closed), with its smooth, aerodynamic bodywork was equipped with 1500cc and then 1600cc pushrod engines in most cases. However, a few were made with a 1588cc twin-overhead-camshaft unit which required too much tender loving care for the average owner with a rather heavy right foot. The MGA handled well and attracted 100,000 buyers before it was replaced by the classic MGB in 1962. This looked a bigger car than its predecessor, but in fact the only item which had been enlarged was the engine, which now boasted 1800cc. Performance and handling of the B have always been adequate rather than electrifying, but the car (which has also been offered with a 3.5-litre V8, and as the MGC with a 3-litre straight-six) has had wide appeal and remained in production

until the demise of the MG factory in 1980.

The GN cyclecar was so popular before World War I that it was made under licence in France by Salmson from 1919 to 1922. Salmson soon decided that the cyclecar was a dying breed, however, and launched their own four-cylinder light sports car with a two-seat body and an overhead-valve, 1100cc power unit. This little machine achieved racing success and the best of the line was the twin-overhead-camshaft Grand Prix of 1926, variants of which were more than a match for the Amilcar CGSs models.

By this time the term 'sports car' was in common use, having been coined by *The Autocar* magazine in 1919. Thus described, such cars began to proliferate, with some distinctly unsporting manufacturers turning out very respectable sporting machinery. One such example was

The Alvis 12/50 was a very popular road car, but it also aquitted itself very well on the track. This is a 12/50 at Boulogne in 1928.

the Hillman sportster of 1919, a much modified version of the 11.9 hp tourer. With Hillman's own polished aluminium bodywork and an outside copper exhaust pipe, this machine very much looked the part, but its speed was somewhat pedestrian. Nevertheless racing editions were successful and it was with one, called *Quick Silver*, that the famous Raymond Mays started his competition career.

This interest in sports cars encouraged some new manufacturers to enter the fray. One such was the British concern Alvis, who quickly followed their first car, the 1500cc 10/30 of 1920, with the slightly smaller but bigger-engined 11/40. These were both sporting cars, but it was their successor, the pushrod-engined 12/50 which, after a hesitant start with the company going into a receiver's hands, captured the sales and the fame and remained in production from 1923 to 1932. The most common body on this fine little 1.5-litre car was a polished aluminium structure from the coachbuilders Cross & Ellis. This featured a 'duck's back' which, along with the somewhat similar 'boat tail', became popular in the 1920s. A new six-cylinder sports tourer

appeared in 1932, known as the Speed Twenty. This was powered by the 2.5-litre engine of the Silver Eagle (itself a variant of the 12/50) and was capable of over 80 mph. In 1937 the engine was enlarged to 3.5 litres for the slightly changed Speed 25, which was really the last true sporting Alvis. The company subsequently turned to tourers like the TC21 of 1953, before amalgamating with Rover in 1965.

Lea-Francis had existed before the war, but car production did not start in earnest until 1921 and it was not until 1925 that the first real sporting car emerged from the company. In fact this, the 12/40 L-type, powered by a 1.5-litre Meadows pushrod engine, bore a remarkable resemblance to the 12/50 Alvis, with a similar duck's back body style. This was not altogether surprising, however, because this too had coachwork by Cross & Ellis. This model was steadily improved, although racing success was rare, and

The graceful Alvis Speed Twenty drop-head tourer was introduced in 1932 powered by a 2.5-litre, six-cylinder engine and capable of more than 80 mph. This car was built in 1934.

the sporting series culminated in the S-type, better known as the Hyper Sports, which had a Cozette supercharger. Although a little unreliable, this 1928 model was a splendid car, the two-seat version being capable of 90 mph.

One company which took advantage of the immediate post-war boom was Alfa Romeo (Nicola Romeo had taken over the factory in 1914). The Italian company's first post-war car – incidentally the first true Alfa Romeo and the last car to be designed by Giuseppe Merosi – was the RL of 1922. This was a basic touring car, but there were also sporting RLS and RLSS versions. The RLSS of 1925 had a shortened chassis which was usually clothed in an open body. Powered by an 83 bhp, 2994cc, six-cylinder engine with pushrod-operated valves and dry-sump lubrication, it was capable of 85 mph in two-seater form and was extremely successful in competition.

Vittorio Jano took over the design team when Merosi left and his first effort was the glorious P2 racer. However, he did not neglect the production side and his 6C1500 of 1927 owed much to the P2. Three versions of this were available,

all with a six-cylinder, 1500cc engine equipped either with one or two overhead camshafts. The top model, the Super Sport also had a supercharger and could manage 90 mph. The engines were enlarged in 1929 to 1750cc and the same variants were available, with the addition of a Gran Sport model which could top the 100 mph mark. In 1931 a new eight-cylinder engine was introduced, a delightful unit with two four-cylinder blocks and a ten-bearing crankshaft; the twin-cam unit was also supercharged and had an initial capacity of 2300cc, which rose to 2600cc soon after. The bodywork was little different from that of the 6C.

In 1935 the P3 racers were swept away by the might of Mercedes and Auto Union, so Alfa Romeo were left with a large number of racing engines. Jano modified these for road use, by enlarging them to 2.9 litres and detuning them in

other ways. Even in this form the eight-cylinder units produced 180bhp and they found homes in superb bodywork by Touring of Milan. To many this was *the* classic Alfa.

After World War II a new 6C2500 was produced, supposedly in sporting form, but despite a 105 bhp engine it was nothing special by Alfa standards. The withdrawal of the company from Grand Prix racing at the end of the 1951 season led to a change in policy. In 1954 a new sporting saloon, the 1300cc, twin-cam Giulietta was announced and this was joined by the larger Giulia. These were very much in the Alfa Romeo tradition of handling and performance and many versions, including open 'spiders' were produced. In fact a spider was listed by the company until nearly the end of the 1970s, by which time it had a 2-litre engine.

The last real sports car to come from Alfa Romeo was the short-lived Montreal of 1970. This had a sleek GT (in the modern sense) body on a 1750 saloon floor pan and was powered by a front-mounted 2.5-litre, four-cam V8 (developed from that of the T33 racer). It performed well, but it was never a big seller and was withdrawn in 1976.

The Alfa Romeo 6C owed much of its design to the racing P2. A good car was made even better in 1929 when the engine was enlarged to 1750cc, as in the car shown here.

The end of the 1920s brought the hardship of the Depression years, which caused sports cars – a luxury rather than a utility – to lose appeal; people needed sensible family cars, if at all. However, those companies which survived developed some classic sports cars during the period up to the second war.

One great company which moved smoothly out of the Vintage period in 1930 was Bugatti. As we have previously seen, most Bugattis owed a great deal to racing practice and some – such as the Type 55 – combined the engine of one car with the chassis of another (in this case the 51 engine with the 54 chassis). First produced in 1931, the Type 55 was reckoned to be one of the finest sports cars ever, with its blown 2.3-litre, double-overhead-camshaft straight-eight and elegant two-seat body giving a maximum speed of 115 mph. However, the most classic Bugatti road car was surely the Type 57 of 1934, powered

Until the end of the 1970s it was an Alfa Romeo tradition to offer a convertible or 'spider'. The car depicted here is a 1750cc Spider Veloce of 1969.

Bugatti's Type 57 was available in various guises; this is the SC, with a shortened chassis and a supercharged 220 bhp engine to give a maximum of 130 mph.

Jean Bugatti's incredible electron alloy body for the Type 57 Atlantic Coupé. It seems that of 750 Type 57s built, only four were thus equipped.

by a supercharged 3.3-litre, double-overhead-camshaft straight-eight. This was a particularly good model, because it was less temperamental than others and Ettore had for the first time taken the necessity for maintenance into account in his design. Also, his son Jean was deeply involved in the 57 and his influence was clearly seen in some of the body styles. Sports versions consisted of the 1935 57S, with shortened chassis and 185 bhp (as against the standard 135) and the 57SC, with a supercharged 220 bhp engine and 130 mph maximum. One of the stranger bodies to come from Jean's pen was the Atlantic Coupé, built of magnesium alloy and held together by an ugly rivetted external flange down the centre of the car.

This was the last car to come from *le Patron*, as Ettore was universally known. Jean was killed in 1939, while testing a car, then the Germans took over the factory during the war and after a long struggle with the post-war French Government which finally resulted in the return of the Molsheim works, the old man died disillusioned in 1947. A subsequent revival of the company

was not a success, despite the eventual production of a new model.

We have already looked at sporting Austins, but it is not generally known that BMW (Bayerische Motoren Werke) started out by acquiring Dixi, the German company building Austin Sevens under licence. BMW continued production of this machine, but also developed a new car, the 303, with a 1200cc, six-cylinder engine. This unit, by now in 2-litre form, found a home in 1936 in the famous sports 328. The power output of the engine, with its ingenious cross-over pushrod system opening inclined valves, was impressive at an initial 80 bhp. The car combined a light, streamlined open body with excellent handling and could manage 100 mph. It remained in production until 1940.

The BMW car factory fell into East German hands after the war, so it took the company some

A front view of the Atlantic Coupé, so readily distinguished by its ugly external rivetted seams. This rare car was built in 1938.

time to convert the motor cycle works for car production, which did not restart until 1952. The first post-war sports car was the sleek 507 of 1955, with a 3.2-litre V8. Based on a shortened 501 saloon chassis and with an open or closed two-seat body, the 507 was capable of more than 135 mph. Unfortunately, though, it was too expensive compared with the Mercedes 300SL and only 250 had been built by the time it was discontinued in 1959.

There were no more true sports cars until the M1 of the 1970s, powered by a four-valve, 3.5-litre straight-six, which only then came about as a result of BMW taking over a design that the troubled Lamborghini concern could not produce. This was never intended as a volume production car, however, and was perhaps most noted for its performance in the BMW-sponsored Procar championship for top racing drivers.

As we saw in the last chapter, BMW 328 engines were used by Bristol and AC after World War II, However, Frazer Nash, whose chain-drive sports cars were then famous, were quick to

see the promise of the 328 and so took out a licence to produce it in Britain as the Frazer Nash-BMW. By the end of the war, the AFN company (as Frazer Nash had become) had become involved with the Bristol project, but 1949 saw a new Frazer Nash, still with the 328 engine (by now Bristol-built). This High Speed Model was raced at Le Mans and was soon rechristened the Le Mans Replica. The same applied to the sleeker Mille Miglia coupé and sundry others. For 1953 there was a new Le Mans hardtop coupé, with 150 bhp and optional de Dion suspension. All the Frazer Nashes of this period were Bristol-BMW powered and production ceased in 1956, by which time AFN were the British Porsche concessionaires.

Meanwhile, the other half of GN, H. R. Godfrey, had formed HRG in 1935. Surprisingly, the initials were not all his; his partners

were E. A. Halford and G. H. Robins and their joint aim was to build cars in the Frazer Nash tradition – simple, effective and with the accent on pure performance. Their first car was a 1.5-litre Meadows-engined two-seater which had excellent roadholding but felt as though the springs had been forgotten by the designers. The Meadows engine was becoming outmoded, so HRG adopted 1100 and 1500cc Singer units, the latter powering the little car to a good 80 mph. After the war, designs were very similar, but aerodynamic cars were introduced in 1946 on the 1500 base. The flexibility of the chassis made this body fragile and only a few were made. A new aerodynamic car was announced in 1955, with a twin-overhead-cam version of the Singer SM1500 engine, but this was never put into production and the company switched to general engineering in 1956.

Singer themselves dabbled in sports cars in the

BMW's 507 of 1955 was certainly elegant and performed very well. Unfortunately, however, it was too expensive to catch on in the face of competition.

1920s and 1930s. The 848cc Junior was not a particularly successful machine, even in its Porlock form, but the same overhead-cam engine was fitted in the Nine of 1932. A good Le Mans run in 1933 for a version of this led to a production Le Mans car which performed well and was popular. A 1.5-litre, six-cylinder version of the Nine was also offered, capable of 100 mph or so, but after the war the 1.5-litre SM roadster was a considerably watered down successor to the earlier sports cars.

By the mid-1930s, Morgan were producing Ford Eight-engined three-wheelers alongside the twins and 1935 saw the announcement of the first four-wheeler, called the 4/4. This inherited many of the three-wheeler's proven assets, such as the sliding-pillar independent front suspension and a gearbox separate from the engine. Powered by an 1122cc Coventry Climax engine, the two-seater 4/4 was joined by a four-seat model in 1937. In the following year the 1267cc Standard 10 engine was fitted and after the war this gave way to the 2-litre Standard Vanguard unit for the new Plus Four. Triumph 2-litre TR engines came in 1952, but Morgans remained basically the same, with simple ladder chassis and ash-framed body. Externally, a curved radiator replaced the flat item and the separate wings merged into the front bodywork, but little else was altered. The end of the four-cylinder TRs brought the Ford 1600 engine in the 1960s and the 3.5-litre V8-engined Plus Eight joined the range in 1968, with electrifying performance. An unusual coupé, the Plus-Four-Plus, with glass-fibre bodywork, was tried in the 1960s, but only fifty were built.

Special bodies were popular on Austin Seven chassis and Swallow built some of the finest before turning to complete car manufacture. We have already looked at SS saloons, but 1935 saw the introduction of the sports SS90, a short-wheelbase version of the SS1 with a side-valve 2.5-litre Standard engine and low sports bodywork. For the following year there was the SS100, with a new overhead-valve version of the power unit and better suspension. The real classic was the 3.5-litre edition, surely one of the most elegant sports cars of all time and capable – at last – of 100 mph.

The BMW M1 coupé of the late 1970s was BMW's first sporting effort for twenty years and it came about through liaison with Lamborghini.

As with several other companies, Singer named a car after the Le Mans 24-hour race in which it had performed well. In this case the car was the two-seat Nine of 1933.

When this 1.5-litre HRG was built in 1948 the company had already introduced an aerodynamic design to complement its range. However, this proved fragile, so the earlier car continued.

Morgan's first four-wheeled car, known as the 4/4, was announced in 1935, with an 1122cc Coventry Climax engine. This car was the reserve for the 1938 Le Mans team.

The aerodynamic Morgan Plus-Four-Plus represented a complete departure for Morgan in 1963. However, Morgan lovers wanted tradition and only fifty of the glassfibre coupés were produced.

After the war, Jaguar (for this is what the company became in 1945, having already used Jaguar as a model name) waited until 1948 to unleash its next bombshell – the twin-overhead-camshaft, 3.4-litre, six-cylinder XK120. This and the later saloons set the style for all Jaguars that followed. All have borne an obvious Jaguar line. The two-seat open or closed machine, named after its engine type and its top speed, was later supplanted by the XK140 and 150 models, with more power, greater sophistication and higher speed. Racing versions, the C- and D-types were victorious five times at Le Mans and the XKSS, which was closely based on the D-type, was to be Jaguar's next sports car. As it turned out, a fire at the factory in Coventry destroyed the tools for this machine and a change of policy led instead to the ubiquitous E-type of 1961.

After World War II it was very much a case of 'as you were' in car manufacture. There was no post-war boom, as there had been in 1919; on the contrary, depressed times and rationing went on for many years. With many car factories destroyed by bombing and plenty of others turned over to the production of munitions, car production was slow to restart. Even when it did, it was mainly pre-war models which filled the catalogues.

One of the first *new* post-war makes was Healey. Donald Healey was already a noted

The 3.5-litre engine turned the SS100 into a 100mph sports car in 1937. Sadly production ceased when war came, although this car was specially built for Ian Appleyard in 1946.

competition driver and had been designer for Triumph. In 1946 he built the first car to bear his own name, powered by the 104 bhp, 2.5-litre Riley engine and available either as a two-seat saloon or as a four-seat roadster. With advanced streamlined styling, the Healey was capable of 105 mph in closed form. In 1949, however, came the more famous Silverstone model, based on the same chassis, but with a stark and purposeful open two-seat body. This was successful on the track, but Jaguar's new XK120 comprehensively put paid to its chances of a roaring production success.

After turning out a Nash-engined machine for the American market in 1950, Healey produced his greatest creation for the 1952 London Motor Show. This was known as the Healey 100 and it attracted such attention at the show that Sir Leonard Lord, boss of Austin, realised that Healey would never be able to cope with production. Thus was born the Austin-Healey partnership and the Austin-Healey 100. Powered by the 2.7-litre, four-cylinder Austin A90 engine, the car went into production in 1953 and was soon joined in the range by the tuned 100S,

The Healey Silverstone, which first appeared in 1949, achieved success on the race track, but it was completely overshadowed in production by the Jaguar XK120.

Considered by many to be the last of the true sports cars, the Austin-Healey 3000 was built until 1968. Here Timo Makinen and Paul Easter are seen in the 1965 RAC Rally.

with 132 bhp in place of the normal 90. In 1956
the 2.6-litre Austin six-cylinder power unit was
dropped into a slightly enlarged body to make the
100/6 and three years later, with an extra 300cc,
the name was changed to 3000. By now the car
was capable of over 120 mph and was steadily
further refined, mainly in the areas of creature
comfort, finally going out of production in
Mk III form in 1968.

The Healey name had also been used from
1958 for the little Sprite, powered by the 948cc
A-series engine and so readily identifiable by its
bulging bonnet-mounted headlamps which
brought about its nickname 'Frog eye'. In 1961 a
more conventional front end was fitted and an
MG Midget variant added to the range and with
various other modifications along the way the
model survived until 1980.

Donald Healey's final effort came in the form
of an alliance with Jensen to build the Jensen-
Healey, a two-seat sports car powered by the
Lotus 2-litre, four-cylinder unit. Announced in
1972, the new Healey never really came up to
expectations and when financial troubles finally
closed Jensen down, the little sports car went
with them.

Although the name was the same, Lea-Francis
was a rather different animal in the post-war
years. The company had changed hands in 1937,
after a period in receivership, and the likes of the
Hyper were not seen again. A new 1.5-litre, four-
cylinder engine was designed by Hugh Rose, who
was also responsible for Riley's similar high-cam
engine, and this was fitted to a new sports car.
The war interrupted production, but in 1947 a
new two-seater was announced, also powered by
the four-cylinder unit, and three years later this
was followed by the 18 hp, with a 2.5-litre engine.
Although the 18 was a good car, it could not keep
the company going for long and it was the last
important model made.

Also soldiering on after the war was AC, but it
was 1953 before a new sports car, the Ace,
appeared. This had a new tubular chassis and the

*Jaguar's remarkable XK120 was replaced in 1954
by the updated XK140, which was externally
distinguished by a central chrome strip and proper
bumpers.*

Previous page: when Lea-Francis introduced the 2.5-litre-engined model in 1950, it was something of a final fling: manufacturing costs were simply climbing too high. This 1956 car was one of the last.

old 2-litre six. Clothed in a pretty two-seat open body, the Ace could manage over 100 mph and from 1956 it was available with the 2-litre Bristol engine, itself eventually supplanted by the Ford Zodiac 2.6-litre unit. The Ace was supplemented by the V8-engined Cobra in 1962, but this belongs in a later chapter.

In the 1970s AC announced a new mid-engined, 3-litre sports two-seater known as the ME3000. After an enormously long gestation period, this Ford-powered machine was just about in production in 1980, but although it was well made, it was not very well received by the press and very few cars were seen on the roads.

The period around World War II was one in which many enthusiasts were building their own specials for use in trials. Sidney Allard began his manufacturing career in this way in the 1930s, but by the time war came he was turning out

practical road-going sports cars with Lincoln Zephyr 4.4-litre V12s. After the war, the company built a whole series of American-engined sports cars and tourers, the most notable of which was the short-chassis two-seater known as the J2 and powered by a 4.4-litre Mercury V8. With de Dion rear suspension, the J2 handled well and with an overhead-valve conversion to push the power output to 140 bhp, 110 mph was possible.

Allard sports cars were in competition with the likes of Triumph, who, in 1953, started production of the TR2. The original TR1 was a prototype exhibited at the 1952 London Motor Show and this was modified to become the production TR2. The basis of the car was a Standard Eight chassis with a 2-litre, four-cylinder Standard Vanguard engine. Even in this form the car was capable of 115 mph, but it was soon upgraded to become the TR3 and then the TR3A, with more power and disc brakes, and

Probably the best known of the Allards was the J2, powered by a 4.4-litre Mercury V8 engine. This 1950 car is seen at a Prescott hill-climb in 1953.

with more room inside. In 1961 a new Michelotti body was added for the TR4, which also had a 2.1-litre engine. An 'A' suffix was again added in 1965 when independent rear suspension became standard, although this was not a popular move at the time among enthusiasts, as it was felt that the handling was degraded. Despite this the TR4A was a good seller. The 2.5-litre, six-cylinder, fuel-injected power unit was fitted in 1968, when the Triumph became the TR5, but very few of these were produced before the car was again reskinned to take the title TR6.

This family line culminated in 1976 with the announcement of the all-new TR7. Initially in hard-top coupé form only, the TR7 was powered by the 2-litre, four-cylinder Triumph Dolomite engine (without the four-valve head used by the Sprint). Although the handling was felt to be superb, there was no excess of power and the announcement of a 3.5-litre V8 version was greeted with joy. Although this was never made available in Great Britain, it was common in the United States and was very successful in rallying. The drop-head version of 1979 gave the TR7 some real style which it had, in the eyes of many, previously lacked. Sadly, US sales of the TR7 did

The exceptionally sleek Aston Martin DB2 was introduced in 1950, with a new twin-overhead-camshaft six-cylinder engine. This rare drop-head was made in 1953.

not come up to expectations and BL announced that the model was to be dropped in 1981, leaving the company with no sports car in its range for the first time in memory.

Like BMC, Triumph had also offered a small sports car, in this case the Spitfire, based on Herald mechanical parts and fitted with a pretty two-seat body. This was announced in 1963 and was joined in 1967 by the fast-back GT6 – basically the same car, but powered by the 2-litre, six-cylinder Vitesse engine. Both cars went through several marks and the Spitfire continued into 1980 before being discontinued.

Like Lea-Francis, Aston Martin was a new company after World War II. David Brown took over in 1947 and in 1948 the concern produced the DB1, with a particularly fine tubular chassis and a 2-litre, four-cylinder engine. Two years later the DB2 followed, with a shorter chassis and a new 2.6-litre, twin-overhead-camshaft six

The DB4 of 1959 marked the beginning of a new line of Astons. The lightweight 'Superleggera' body by Touring of Milan housed a new 240bhp, 3.7-litre six.

designed by W. O. Bentley for Lagonda (by now also part of Aston Martin). The body was a sleek closed coupé, as were most of the DB series, which continued through to the DBS of 1968. The DB3S of 1955 had 3 litres and a top speed of 150 mph, open or closed, while disc brakes appeared on the 3.7-litre DB4 four years later. Once again the engine size was increased in 1964, when the 4-litre DB5 appeared, closely followed by the slightly altered DB6. A Vantage engine has been available for several of the Astons, this being the company's name for a more powerful version (although power outputs are never quoted). Volante is the name for convertibles and one of the most stylish of these is a version of the Aston Martin V8. This started life in 1968 as the DBS, powered by the six-cylinder engine, but a new 5.3-litre, four-cam V8 was soon introduced and the DB part of the name disappeared when David Brown dropped out. The V8 is the only Aston Martin of 1980, although it is offered in several forms, including the Vantage.

The most famous sporting name in post-war France is Alpine, founded by Jean Rédélé in 1955. The company has concentrated on Renault-engined cars and has, in fact, been owned since 1974 by Renault. The most note-

worthy Alpine by far has been the A110 Berlinette, built from 1963 to 1977 and a highly successful rally car. It had a tubular backbone chassis and a glassfibre body. The size of the rear-mounted engine varied from 956cc to 1796cc, although the most popular version was fitted with the 1300cc Renault R8 unit. In rally trim, with the 1800 engine, the A110 could manage 135 mph and ownership of such a machine has been the ambition of many a young Frenchman.

Just as the Alpine A110 has been the ultimate sports car to the French, so Porsche's 911 has been to German enthusiasts. Porsche's first car to bear his name was the 356, which appeared in 1948 as a special-bodied VW with the engine turned round. To gain luggage space, however, it was turned back for production cars and the capacity was also reduced to 1100cc. Mostly sold in closed form, the 356 was steadily modified over the years, but remained the same basic car until its demise in 1965. The 911 was introduced in

1964, with a new air-cooled flat six of 2 litres fitted at the rear as before. When the 356 was dropped, its engine, by now a 1600, was put into the 911 body to form the 912. Even in basic form the 911 could manage 120 mph, but there has been a mass of variants, mostly closed, but some with removable 'Targa' roof panels. For many years the 911S was the fastest version, but the 1970s brought the even quicker Carrera and Turbo models featured in the final chapter.

In 1976 an all-new Porsche was announced, powered by a front-mounted, water-cooled Audi 2-litre four and driven through a rear-mounted transaxle. This was the 924, a sort of poor man's Porsche with somewhat mundane performance but superb handling. The Turbo version of 1979 restored the balance, however, By this time Porsche were also marketing the 4.5-litre V8-engined 928. This 240 bhp engine, again water-cooled and front-mounted, was fitted to a curvaceous 2 + 2 body and was enlarged to 4.7

litres for the 928S of 1979, which was hailed as a truly splendid motor car.

Porsche, to most people, means exotic machines, and the same applies to Ferrari, revered the world over by red-blooded motorists. The vast majority of Ferrari road cars have been built with twelve-cylinder engines, indeed Enzo Ferrari was reputed to have said that any engine with fewer cylinders could not be a true Ferrari. The earliest machines set the pattern in the form of three series of cars beginning with the 2-litre type 166 of 1948 and progressing through the 2.3-litre type 195 to the 2.6-litre type 212 of 1950. The new 4.1-litre V12 of 1951 was fitted to a run of road cars which culminated in 1955 with the

Tadek Marek must surely have been influenced by Jaguar's famous XK engine when he designed the all aluminium double-overhead-camshaft six for Aston Martin in the late 1950s.

The Alpine A110 was a highly successful racing and rally car and was built for nearly 15 years. This is the 1600S version of 1970, with a tuned Renault 16 engine.

The ultimate development of Porsche's 911 series of cars was the Turbo model, initially powered by a 3-litre flat-six, later enlarged to 3.3 litres.

The air-cooled, horizontally opposed six of the Porsche Turbo, with the turbocharger clearly visible at bottom right. This is an early unit without an intercooler.

Fiat made use of Ferrari's splendid V6 Dino engine in the front of their neat Pininfarina roadster, also called the Dino. This is the spider version of 1969.

rare and beautiful Superfast, which was not actually as fast as its name suggested.

Despite the Commendatore's assertion regarding twelve-cylinder engines, he produced a new V6-engined 206 Dino in 1967, based on an earlier racing configuration and named after his late son, Alfredino. This was the first road-going Ferrari to have a mid-mounted engine and it was dressed in a superbly elegant Pininfarina skin, usually closed but with a removable roof panel in the 'Spider' version. After growing from 2 litres to 2.4 litres for the 246 Dino, the model was replaced by an all-new 2+2 308GT Dino in 1974. This Bertone-bodied model was equipped with a 3-litre V8, which was also found in the two-seat Pininfarina version of the car, the 308GTB. The latter model was special because it was the first Ferrari to have glassfibre bodywork, not that this lasted long, the company soon reverting to metal, even for the 308.

Ferrari have been owned by Fiat for some years, and even before this there was a certain amount of co-operation. The V6 Dino engine was slightly detuned and used in the front of Fiat's own Dino, also styled by Pininfarina but usually convertible. However, Fiat's first post-war sports car was the beefy 8V two-seat coupé, powered by a 2-litre V8. Although it performed well, with a maximum speed of 120 mph, the 8V was a highly specialised venture which could not economically be maintained by a giant like Fiat. Fiat's most recent sports offering is the Bertone-styled X1/9, with a Targa-roofed body powered by, originally, the 1300cc 128 engine transversely mounted behind the two seats. Handling was fine from the start, but performance was disappointing, so that 1500cc Ritmo/Strada was dropped in during 1978 and this, together with a five-speed gearbox, made a considerable difference.

Maserati has a history longer than that of Ferrari, yet has not maintained the glitter. We have already looked at the company's first true road car, the A6GCS and at the four-door Quattroporte, but a series of front-engined road

Porsche's 356 started life in 1948 as a special-bodied VW and remained in production until 1965, when it was replaced by the 912, a four-cylinder version of the 911.

A Daimler SP250 of 1960. The styling was controversial, with glassfibre bodywork, but there was no doubt that the SP was a true sports car, killed only by Jaguar's takeover.

Opposite page: surely one of the most classic sports cars of all time – Ferrari's 246 Dino, styled by Pininfarina and named after Enzo's dead son.

cars was also produced. In 1957 the 3500GT emerged, powered by a 3.5-litre, twin-cam six. This was followed by the similar 5000GT in 1959 and the 3.7-litre, six-cylinder Mistrale in 1963. The Ghibli started a new generation of Maseratis with its four-cam 4.7-litre V8, but this was still front-mounted, as it was in the 4.1-litre Vignale four-seat-bodied Indy (named after success at that legendary track). However, then the engine finally moved backwards for the Bora of 1971, of which more later. During the 1970s Citroën took

over and then ditched Maserati, but during the short marriage emerged the smaller, lighter version of the Bora, known as the Merak and fitted with a 3-litre, four-cam V6 designed by Maserati for the unique Citroën SM. Citroën's ownership of the company brought their strange pneumatic braking system to the Merak, but this indelicate and unpopular arrangement was replaced at the end of the decade, *post*-Citroën.

The third corner of the Italian high-performance triangle is Lamborghini. Unlike the other two, this company has not developed its road cars out of a sporting background: Ferruccio Lamborghini, a tractor maker, is reputed to have entered car manufacture because he was dissatisfied with the service he obtained from Ferrari. He had a 3.5-litre, four-cam V12 designed by Bizzarini and fitted it at the front of the 3500GT coupé announced at the 1965 Turin Show. This was a fine and fast machine which

handled well. In 1966 its engine was enlarged to 4 litres and a 2 + 2 body was offered. The most famous Lamborghini came in 1967 in the form of the mid-engined Miura, but this, along with the stunning Countach and other supercars, belongs in the final chapter.

There has been a succession of 2 + 2 and four-seat Lamborghinis and just about all of them – Islero, Marzal, Jarama, Espada – have been powered by the 4-litre V12. The exception has been the Urraco, also a 2 + 2 but powered by a mid-mounted V8, at first of 2.5 litres and subsequently a full 3 litres. The company has had something of a troubled existence, but the quality of its cars has never suffered as a result.

As the years have passed there has been less room for new sports cars; there has been a trend towards high-performance versions of saloons or luxurious GT cars. At the beginning of the 1960s there were still plenty of manufacturers in the

Lancia's striking Stratos was a rare beast indeed as a road car, but it frequently stole the thunder in rallying. Here, Bjorn Wåldegard competes in the RAC Rally.

sports car field, particularly with a booming 'kit-car' market, but by 1980 legislation and standardisation had killed off the majority of these. Many of the makes continue, but the cars cannot be called sports cars.

One such manufacturer is Daimler, who in 1959 launched a glassfibre-bodied two-seater, powered by the company's 2.5-litre V8 and known as the SP250 or, by some, the Dart. Not universally thought of as handsome, the SP250 nonetheless performed adequately, particularly in B-type form, but Daimler had been acquired by Jaguar and the E-type was sufficient sporting product for the company.

Another V8 sports car of the 1960s was the

Sunbeam Tiger of 1964, which was basically the Rootes Alpine equipped with an American Ford 4.2-litre V8. The car was fine in a straight line, but its handling left a little to be desired.

Most of the Lotus story is one of a kit-car manufacturer, but the 1970s saw a change of direction for this, one of the last true sporting builders. We have already seen the Elite sports saloon, but Lotus have not deserted the two-seat market altogether, for the Esprit, with its mid-mounted 2-litre (now 2.2), four-cylinder engine and wind-cheating Giugiaro styling is a real sports car, with the traditionally excellent Lotus handling and roadholding. The range was augmented in 1980 by a turbocharged version of the car, specially built from the ground up and finished in the livery of the company's Formula one sponsors.

That year also saw the revival of Lancia's Monte Carlo, a mid-engined machine based on the mechanical parts of the Beta 2000. This had perhaps always been somewhat overshadowed by the 'homologation special' Stratos (400 had to be built to make it eligible for competition in Group 4). Again mid-engined, this striking two-seater was powered by the revived Fiat Dino engine (Fiat also own Lancia), and was enormously successful in rallying.

The first appearance of the Wankel engine in a production car was in the sporting NSU Wankel Spyder, which appeared in the early 1960s as a roadster version of the Sport Prinz. Since then, however, NSU have given up Wankel production, the fine Ro80 saloon having cost the company a lot of money, and the banner has been taken up by the Japanese Mazda concern, who in 1980 were producing a very elegant 2 + 2 coupé called the RX7. Equipped with a front-mounted twin-rotor Wankel with an equivalent capacity of 2.3 litres and a power output of 105 bhp, the RX7 was an exceptionally quick machine which also 'cleaned up' in motor racing. The Wankel was at one time seen by many as the great white hope of motoring, but NSU's problems with the engine changed all this. However, Mazda seemed to have surmounted many snags, such as that of high rotor tip wear rates and equally high fuel consumption.

The end of the 1970s saw an ever worsening situation for sports car enthusiasts; so many great names had either gone or had changed their approach completely. For many aficionados the closure of MG's famous Abingdon factory in 1980 was the final nail in the coffin.

AMERICAN IDEAS

A real boy-racer's car, this Plymouth Roadrunner Superbird of 1970 is bedecked with devices that make it look fast, but has nothing special under the bonnet.

All the cars looked at so far have originated in Europe or Japan, and there has been a certain common background, in terms of early competitions and similar conditions and requirements, to encourage a harmonious theme. In the far-off pioneering days of motoring, the United States had its own peculiar set of problems to pose for the motorist and so sports car development began on a somewhat special footing.

As we have already found, most of Europe's sports cars of the pre-World War I period were road-going variants of racing machines. In contrast, most of the early American sports cars were evolved from tourers and saw competition only when enterprising agents decided that such an airing would do sales no harm. The condition of the roads in the States was basic, to say the least: where there was any attempt at surfacing, which was generally only in urban areas, the materials used were very crude and the result of only limited success. As for the country roads, these were little more than dirt tracks, better suited to hoofs than to wheels, and maintenance was universally neglected, so that pot-holes were the rule rather then the exception.

America is such a massive tract of land that plenty of power has always been desirable for long-distance travel. What is more, this size meant that it was many years before any manufacturer had anything like a comprehensive network of dealers capable of carrying out servicing or repairs; the most experienced mechanical repair man in a country district was likely to be thoroughly conversant with the workings of agricultural equipment, but a motor car would cause untold confusion. All these factors together led to a type of car which had plenty of strength to cope with the roads, light weight for nimble handling, a large, powerful engine for muscle (lowly stressed for reliability), and an overall simplicity to facilitate home repairs.

This breed was America's first sporting type, crude yet attractive vehicles consisting usually of little more than a chassis housing two seats and an engine. Names were various – Speedster, Roadster, Runabout, Raceabout – but the style was unmistakable and, like the British Mini half a century later, it appealed to members of all classes, either as a plaything or as a serious mode of transport.

By far the most famous examples of this type of machine were made by Mercer and Stutz. The Mercer company was founded in 1909, and remained in being until the mid-1920s, but it is for one model that the Mercer name is now remembered. Strangely, that model, known as the Raceabout, was only one of a series known as the Type 35, and introduced in 1910. There were five or six versions of the 35, all designed by Finlay Robertson Porter – some in the same stark idiom as the Raceabout and others with full weather protection and even such niceties as doors. The Raceabout version did not in fact appear until 1911 and by 1915 it was gone, but it left an indelible mark on motoring history. Like so many of the speedster machines, the Raceabout was powered by a large, lazy engine, in this case a 4.9-litre, four-cylinder unit with a power output of around 55 bhp. With almost non-existent bodywork and a consequent all-up weight of around a ton, the Raceabout was capable of over 70 mph. The ride was exceptionally firm, the handling nothing special and the brakes apparently left a fair amount to be desired. Nevertheless, there were thousands of owners who were prepared to put up with these pitfalls and with a rather fragile chassis which needed welding from time to time. In 1915, a new range of models replaced the Type 35 and although there was a Raceabout, this was a far more civilised vehicle and did not have the basic appeal of the 35. The company struggled on until 1925, when it finally succumbed.

Despite the taunts of Mercer fans that 'You have to be nuts to drive a Stutz', the Stutz company was actually far longer lived than was Mercer. Harry Stutz built his first car, albeit a very primitive one, in 1897, but it was an extremely reliable run into eleventh place in the first Indianapolis race of 1911 that brought Stutz a flurry of demand for replicas of that racer and gave Harry the slogan 'The car that made good in a day'. Shortly after this, three models were listed by Stutz, powered by a 6.3-litre, four-cylinder engine, producing 60 bhp. By the time the roadster became the legendary Bearcat in 1914, an alternative engine, a straight-six of almost the same capacity and the same power output was offered. Like the Raceabout, which by this time

The Mercer Raceabout of 1910 was just one of the Type 35 series. Here, racer Ralph de Palma is seen in 1911, with Dorothy Lane.

had passed its zenith, the Bearcat had extremely primitive bodywork and at a single glance from the uninitiated might have been the same car. Primitive or not, however, the Bearcat could manage 80 mph in the hands of a brave man and it was extremely reliable, having the unusual features of a three-speed gearbox mounted in unit with the rear axle, considered by many in the 1980s to be an aid to good handling. After the war, Harry Stutz left the company bearing his name to found a new concern, HCS, and the Bearcat changed beyond recognition. The gear-box moved to the conventional position behind the engine, and like later Mercers the Bearcat acquired a completely new body style with such

niceties as a windscreen, a hood and doors.

In 1932 the Bearcat name was revived for the short-chassis version of a six-cylinder saloon known as the Black Hawk. Shortly after this, yet another Bearcat was announced, this time with the subtitle DV32, powered by a brand new eight-cylinder, four-valve engine and sold with a guaranteed maximum speed of 100 mph. There was a shorter-chassised version of this Bearcat

known as the Super Bearcat and the open or closed coupé bodywork was extremely elegant. However, none of these machines had quite the same charisma as the prototype.

Petrol was not the sole source of energy in the bygone days of motoring; indeed many of the earliest motor vehicles were steam powered. In the early part of the century, the Stanley company was renowned for its steamers, which in many cases made their petrol-engined equivalents seem very inefficient. The first Stanleys were built in 1902, but these were tourers. Nevertheless, 1906 saw the Stanley Steamer take the Land Speed Record at 127.56 mph and shortly afterwards the company offered a sporting machine known as the Gentleman's Speedy Roadster. This was one of the first American sporting cars, preceding even the Mercer by four years, and its performance was astonishing. Like its petrol successors, the Speedy Roadster had an austere two-seat body, without any weather protection at all. The kerosene-fired multi-tube boiler was mounted under the coffin-shaped front bonnet, while the twin-cylinder, double-acting engine was located at the rear of the vehicle. Strictly speaking, it was the Model H

The Stutz Bearcat, star of a 1919 silent serial, was quite luxurious compared with the primitive earlier models of the same name.

which was known as the Gentleman's Speedy Roadster, having a 20 hp engine, but there was also a 10 hp Model E and a 30 hp Model K and the Model K was by far the most exciting. With a weight of only 15 cwt and the 30 hp engine, the car was capable of 75 mph, which it achieved over a flying half-mile during a trial at Ormond Beach in the United States. Acceleration of the Steamers was generally noticeably better than that of the petrol counterparts, but the drawback with the system was that it was not possible to get into a steam-engined car and drive it away from cold; it took up to several hours to warm the water and this became even less attractive a proposition when electric starters became the norm on internal combustion engines.

It would not be true to say that all American sports cars of the pre-World War I period were exactly in the speedster idiom; there were a few companies, such as Chadwick and Simplex, producing high-quality sports machines, which

This is a short-chassised Stutz DV32 of 1933, known as the Super Bearcat. Open and closed versions were available and a 100 mph top speed was guaranteed.

were civilised by the standards of the Raceabout and the Bearcat. Most of these concerns were rather short-lived, but their products were nevertheless remembered. Chadwick's greatest claim to sporting fame came with the introduction in 1907 of the Chadwick Six, which was fitted with a six-cylinder, 11.2-litre engine and was available in short-chassis form. In this guise, the Six was capable of more than 60 mph and found a certain amount of success in competitions, but the model was particularly famous for being the first car to use a supercharger. Although the standard machine was unblown, a notable racing driver, Willy Haupt, came up with the idea of supercharging the car and in this form its top speed was boosted to nearly 90 mph. Various systems were tried, but although the supercharged Six saw a great deal of use on the race track it was never put into production.

Despite its involvement in World War I, America was remote enough from the action for its industry to continue without great hardship. When war ended, car production soon got back into full swing and designs changed far less drastically than did those in Europe. The 1920s saw a steady development of the pre-war speed-sters; as we have seen the Mercer Raceabout and the Stutz Bearcat grew up and became 'civilised' and, at the same time, mundane as far as the enthusiast was concerned. More and more new speedsters appeared, the vast majority in the post-war style with doors, windscreens and so on. As in Europe, there was a short post-war boom, during which, in a state of extreme optimism, the public bought cars of all shapes and sizes in massive numbers; this demand was sufficient to support the variety of sporting makers which sprang up – but only for a short time. As the boom subsided, so did the interest in the sporting

Overleaf : Buehrig's classic Auburn 851 Speedster appeared in 1935 to revive the company's flagging fortunes. The supercharged eight could carry the car to a 100 mph, but this did not impress enough people.

machinery and as hardship set in so many such companies died.

Motor sport had never played such a major role in sports car design as it had in Europe, but as the 1920s grew older, fewer road-going cars in the States owed any debt to the race track – the sports car was generally a road car for the man who would like to be a racer but lacked either the money or the courage to have a go.

Not all the speedsters died with the post-war boom: perhaps the most notable survivor, apart from Stutz, was Jordan – even if only because of its sustained and unique advertising campaign, which set a style still very closely followed today. In its series of newspaper advertisements, the company appealed to the secret desire of a large number of people and made those people believe that its cars were made for them without ever describing the cars' actual assets. It was the Playboy Speedster of 1919 with which this campaign started, and Jordan found enough continuing success with this car to maintain a speedster in the catalogue until 1929.

There were two or three halcyon years in the late 1920s, during which people in both Europe and America enjoyed general prosperity. These were the days of Bentley's great wins at Le Mans and they also saw the birth of one of America's most famous sports cars of all time – the Auburn Speedster. By the time the 8-90 appeared in 1928, the Auburn company was under the direction of Erret Lobban Cord, whose name was far more famous in connection with the distinguished line of automobiles which bore it. The Speedster was an uprated version of an earlier model, in this case powered by a 90 bhp, 4.5-litre, straight-eight Lycoming engine (Lycoming was another part of the Cord empire) and fitted with a sleek and stylish boat-tailed body – boat-tailed coach-work was popular on both sides of the Atlantic at this time.

In 1929 came the Wall Street Crash and with it depression throughout the civilised world. This period was a large nail in the coffin of many of

Only two of these Duesenberg SSJs were ever built : this one for Gary Cooper and another for Clark Gable. Bodywork of this 125-inch wheelbase car was by La Grande.

The gleaming 320 bhp supercharged straight-eight of Gary Cooper's Duesenberg SSJ. The blower was a centrifugal unit driven off the front of the crankshaft.

America's sporting manufacturers, in some cases disturbing for ever an already shaky equilibrium and in others starting a steady rot. Auburn seemed to slip easily through these two or three years, but despite the extraordinarily low price of cars such as the Speedster, demand fell alarmingly and the Speedster, along with most other models, was dropped in 1930. There was only a short breathing space, however, for the Speedster reappeared in 1932 with minor modifications. Later in the year a new V12-engined Speedster arrived, powered by a 6.8-litre Lycoming unit and still selling for under $1000. Unfortunately, Cord had misjudged the market, for there were simply not enough purchasers for either the eight- or the twelve-cylinder cars to make them profitable. It is possible that the Speedster was a little too expensive for the impecunious enthusiast and too cheap for the highway promenader. Both Speedsters were dropped again in 1934, but the following year saw the appearance of the 851 Speedster, without doubt Auburn's most classic car. Designed by Gordon Buehrig, the 851 had a supercharged

The coffin-nosed Cord 812, a 1937 example, distinguished from the 810 by its supercharger, which boosted performance beyond the magic 100 mph mark.

version of the old eight-cylinder Lycoming engine, this time with a power output of 150 bhp. Every 851 – and the 852 of the following year – carried a plaque on the dashboard guaranteeing that it had been tested at 100 mph before delivery, but neither this nor the car's superbly elegant styling was enough to achieve success in the market place. Auburn simply could not find enough buyers and once again the Speedster was a loss-maker. This time, however, there was to be no salvation and the factory closed its gates for the last time in 1936.

More than anyone else, E. L. Cord is the key to American sports car manufacture in the 1930s: he had acquired with the two Duesenberg brothers, the Duesenberg company in 1926 and Auburn-Cord-Duesenberg were the three names on every red-blooded American's lips in the 1930s.

Whereas Auburns were remarkably cheap, Duesenbergs were extremely expensive. After his takeover of Duesenberg in 1926, Cord instructed the brothers, Fred and August, to make a new car that would rival the best in the world in terms of style, engineering and sheer panache. The result of this was that at the end of 1928 the company unveiled 'The World's Finest Car', the Model J Duesenberg. This was powered by a 6.9-litre straight-eight, again from Lycoming. Unlike the Auburn's engine, however, this unit had twin overhead camshafts to operate four valves in each cylinder and its claimed power output was 265 bhp, giving the Model J a top speed of more than 115 mph. In 1932, the J was joined in the range by the SJ, whose power output was boosted to some 320 bhp by the addition of a crankshaft-driven centrifugal supercharger. In this form, the Duesenberg could manage nearly 130 mph and although it was by no means an outright sports car – far more a luxury tourer – its performance put it streets ahead of many so-called sportsters. Most of the SJs were built on a shortened chassis, but two SSJs were produced in 1935 with an even shorter chassis; one was for Clark Gable and the other for Gary Cooper and these were the nearest thing to true sports cars that Duesenberg made. Those SSJs were special orders, but the Duesenberg was very much a car for the stars: the list of notable owners was extensive.

Cord's most sporting model was also originally intended to be a Duesenberg. Once again styled by Gordon Buehrig, the 810 so impressed E. L. Cord with its somewhat bizarre coffin-nosed styling that he decided to call it a Cord. Like earlier Cords, the 810 was equipped with front-wheel drive, its 125 bhp Lycoming V8 having an extension on the front of its crankshaft to take the flywheel and transmission. Cord saw the 810 as the poor man's Duesenberg, but if this was so, the specification was surprisingly exotic, with such luxuries as pop-up headlamps adapted from aircraft landing lights, variable speed windscreen wipers and a radio. Announced in late 1935, the 810 did not finally get into production until the following year, due to a hold-up in the supply of the complicated pre-selector gearbox. Even when production was achieved there were numerous faults which had to be ironed out and although the styling was popular the public was not prepared to put up with unreliability. In the following year, despite very poor sales of the 810, Cord introduced a supercharged version known as the 812 which was capable of more than 100 mph. However, this was just not enough to save the Cord empire and, along with Auburn and Duesenberg, the ship sank.

With the demise of the Auburn-Cord-Duesenberg triumvirate, America largely forgot about sports cars until some years after World War II. Even then, the trend in motoring on that side of the Atlantic was towards large-engined, softly sprung, lazy machines – not an ideal background for a new sporting breed. When the renaissance came after the war, it was imported cars which formed the spearhead – marques like MG, Triumph and Jaguar, later to become accepted traditional sights on American roads.

It was not until the 1950s that the States saw its first true home-grown sports car of post-war years (the tiny Crosley Hotshot was introduced in 1949, but this was simply a two-seat version of a saloon car). One of the problems was that there was no motor sport in America to encourage the production of such cars; in Europe there was the classic Le Mans 24-hour race, the equally legendary Sicilian Targa Florio and the awesome Mille Miglia, but in America there was no equivalent. European manufacturers were prepared to build cars especially to win such events which often resulted in superb road-going spin-offs; on the other hand, many existing road-going sports cars were adapted to perform admirably in the races.

It was a desire to beat the Europeans at their own game which led wealthy racer and yachtsman Briggs Cunningham to enter his own team of cars at Le Mans in 1950. These were nothing more than Cadillacs, but in the following year, Cunningham went one step further and built his own Chrysler-powered sports cars in an effort to win the race outright. Despite 220 bhp V8 engines and very impressive chassis specifications, the goal was just beyond Cunningham's reach, and a breakdown nearly halfway through the race robbed him of second place. Over the next four years a series of different Cunninghams was prepared for entry at Le Mans, but victory was never achieved and by 1955 Cunningham simply could not afford to run the equivalent of a full works team. However, his racing programme did lead to some extremely elegant road-racing sports cars during those few years. Clothed by Vignale, these machines were capable of nearly 150 mph, but they were very expensive to produce and even more expensive to buy and so only a few ever reached the roads. However, Cunningham's efforts did revive the sporting spirit in American motoring minds.

During the early 1950s there were numerous small companies producing very specialised sports cars, usually built around mass-production V8s (Britain's Allard company was selling around 75 per cent of its J2s in the States at this time, either fitted as standard with a Mercury V8 engine or imported to the States engineless, to be equipped to suit the owner).

The endeavours of Cunningham and all the others were sufficient to encourage Chevrolet to take a close look at the sports car market. What they saw obviously impressed them, because in 1953 they announced the first of the Corvette series. One of the first mass-production cars to be fitted with a glassfibre body, this original Corvette was powered by a 3.7-litre, side-valve, six-cylinder engine known as the Blue Flame, but it was neither very fast nor particularly nimble. In 1955 an optional V8 engine was introduced, a new overhead-valve unit with a capacity of 4.3 litres and a power output of 180 bhp. This helped

the performance a great deal, but it was still to be several years before the handling was really up to par for a sports car. Competition, in the hands of people such as Zora Arkus-Duntov, produced developments such as fuel injection and a limited-slip differential, but it was the Stingray version, announced in 1962, which really marked the coming of age of the Corvette. This had a completely new body, still of glassfibre, with sleek, streamlined styling incorporating pop-up headlamps. Unlike the earlier models, which were all convertibles, the Stingray was offered with the option of an open top or a closed fastback. Still a V8, the engine had a capacity of 5.4 litres and produced 360 bhp. Independent suspension all round improved the handling no end and the adoption of disc front brakes in 1965 brought braking up to scratch. In 1968, the Corvette was again restyled, the Stingray subtitle was dropped, and engine options were now numerous between 5.4 and 7 litres, although American emission regulations meant that the power output was not as great as might be expected from such large units.

Not only has the Corvette been an extremely popular road car during its long life, it has also acquitted itself remarkably well on the race tracks, particularly at Le Mans, where Corvettes have been some of the most reliable runners.

With the success of this attractive and effective Chevrolet, one might expect other manufacturers to have followed suit and produced true sports cars, but this has not been the case. Most of the other 'sporting' machines made in the United States since the 1950s have been glorified saloons of one type or another: some have been nothing more than 'boy racers', while others have been substantially modified saloons, but saloons nevertheless.

Ford in America made an effort to match Chevrolet's achievements when the company launched the Thunderbird in 1954. True, this was a two-seater, available in open or closed form, and true, it was powered by a 4.8-litre V8

Overleaf: Chevrolet first produced a Corvette model, with glassfibre bodywork, in 1953 and twenty years later, when this was built, the much-changed model was still going strong.

Previous page : Ford's two-seater Thunderbird was produced only between 1954 and 1957, when it was replaced by a four-seater ; this is a 1956 example of the smaller car.

engine, but it simply did not have the sporting impact of the Corvette and although it was very popular in its day it could not really compete and it was dropped in 1957, the name being used on a four-seater thereafter. It is fair to say that the Thunderbird sports car was not really given a chance. If Ford had persevered as Chevrolet did, then the T'bird might well have become the Corvette's equal, both on the road and on the track.

The Corvette was not Chevrolet's only sports car of the 1950s and 1960s, for in 1959 came the infamous Corvair, later to be slammed in Ralph Nader's book, *Unsafe At Any Speed*. This was announced as the company's economy car, being their first to have a unitary body/chassis. However, it was very expensive to produce, having a unique air-cooled, horizontally opposed

six-cylinder engine mounted at the rear (which gave the car dubious handling characteristics and gave Nader lead for his pencil). Despite the problems and the expense, a sporting Monza version appeared and some of these even had turbocharged engines. However, although the Monza was latterly more popular than the basic Corvair, sales were just too slow for the company and Nader's campaign was the final twist of the knife.

Initially Ford's famous Mustang of 1964 was a competitor for the Monza, but it soon became clear to Chevrolet that they would have to think again in order to keep up. The Mustang was never a sports car in its standard form, more a sports tourer for the enthusiast. Chassis specification was somewhat basic, but engine options were numerous, ranging from a modest 2.8-litre straight-six to the 4.7-litre V8, as used in the AC Cobra and some versions of the Ford GT40.

The 1974 version of Pontiac's Trans-Am Firebird, which was nothing more than an edition of Chevrolet's excellent Camaro.

Other options were numerous, including hard or soft tops, drum or disc brakes, manual or power-assisted steering and manual or automatic transmission, but all the cars were four-seaters. The Mustang – or Pony Car – proved to be incredibly popular and, somewhat surprisingly, began to achieve success on the race track. This encouraged well known tuning houses to produce their own special versions of the car and perhaps the most notable were Carroll Shelby's machines, which could take on just about all comers.

As with so many other American sporting cars, the heavy weight of legislation in the 1970s changed the Mustang beyond recognition and removed it from the Christmas list of all but the most dedicated aficionados. Nevertheless, the Mustang had achieved immense popularity and so many were sold that it almost became America's Ford Anglia.

When Chevrolet realised that the Monza was losing ground to the Mustang, they hurriedly thought again and came up with the Camaro. Launched in 1966, this was very much a two-door saloon, but like the Mustang, it could be had with remarkable performance, in this case from a 6.5-litre, 330 bhp V8. For those without deep pockets, a smaller six-cylinder engine was available, lacking such niceties as disc brakes, so that even the ordinary man could pretend. Also, like the Mustang, the Camaro has been very successful in saloon racing and for those wanting to be a little different the car has been offered in badge-engineered form as the Pontiac Firebird.

Chevrolet and Ford have not had an exclusive right to sports car manufacture in the United States over the last few years; the American Motors Corporation joined the fray in 1968 with their own rival for the Mustang, known as the Javelin. In Ford style, this could be had with any of a variety of engines, but the most powerful was a 280 bhp, 5.6-litre V8. The Javelin was a two-door, four-seat coupé, but it was soon followed by a shorter two-seat version known as the AMX. In this model, the largest engine available had a capacity of 6.3 litres and gave the car a top speed of nearly 140 mph in standard trim. Like the

Corvette, the AMX was a sports car, but the other American giant was content to uprate its saloon models to satisfy sporting appetites.

Chrysler came into the field with the Dodge Charger which, like so many others, started out as a forty sports saloon, but was watered down as years passed. This also applied to their Challenger model. Another Chrysler company, Plymouth, produced the Barracuda which, with the noted 'Hemi' engine, in which guise it was known as the Hemi-Cuda, was particularly successful. Then in 1970 Plymouth turned to a more superficial sporting image with the Roadrunner Superbird.

One of the better sporting saloons of the 1960s came from Studebaker, who produced their glassfibre Avanti four-seat coupé in 1962. In its optional supercharged form this was a fast car and was successful in competition, but the demise of the Studebaker concern in 1966 brought a premature end to Avanti production, despite the efforts of a dealership, which turned out a few Avanti II variants thereafter.

Punitive legislation not only deterred new American sporting attempts, but proved to be a large millstone for many European manufacturers, who had previously sold a great proportion of their sports car production in the States. At one point it was thought that America was going to ban sales of convertible cars, in a new era of safety consciousness, and this had a disastrous effect on plans for several new European models; indeed it was a key factor in the transition from open roadsters to closed GT cars, such as the new breed of Lotus and the original Triumph TR7. For the small European manufacturer, it was simply too expensive to develop cars to the sort of specification required by American law, simply to satisfy those demands, especially as the end result was generally an inferior machine. However, for those makers with the money or the courage to persevere, the American sports car market has generally remained a lucrative one, the TR7's early demise being attributable to rejection by piqued MG fanciers.

SPECIALIST
SPORTS
CARS

The term 'specialist sports car' is a general one used to describe several different varieties of sporting machine which do not conform in one way or another. This group includes 'specials', popular until the 1950s both for trials use and as everyday transport for the individualist; it also encompasses component cars, offered in kit form in order to reduce the price, and 'replicars' – vehicles built either as exact copies of an earlier famous model or to follow the theme of a particular period.

There were really two types of special: the commercially built machine and the home-brew cobbled up out of a wide range of parts. In fact, most of the commercial offerings have been the result of private efforts attracting enquiries from would-be purchasers. The start of it all was the Austin Seven, which formed the basis of the vast majority of specials built until World War II. Its attraction was that it was cheap and light and yet it was rugged and could be easily encouraged to perform well. The earliest specials involved little more than taking a standard Austin rolling chassis and clothing it in a stark, simple body, often crudely hand-formed from sheet aluminium. Doors and weather protection were unusual, but then these were the days when it was considered *de rigueur* to suffer a certain amount of discomfort in a sports car.

As the years passed, so the specials became more original, sundry modifications being carried out to the base engine and chassis in order to improve performance as much as possible. For road use the machines became more practical, although still usually being as basic as possible, while for employment in trials they were equipped of necessity with a number of items such as twin 'fiddle' brake levers.

In 1935 came the Ford Ten and it soon became apparent that this car, like the Austin thirteen years its senior, could provide plenty of useful parts for specials. By this time, however, these machines were becoming more individual; for instance, it was rare to find an unaltered chassis in

Previous page : announced in 1967, Ginetta's neat and well made G15 was equipped with a Hillman Imp engine and was one of the longer-lived specialist sports cars.

use, as tubular frames were taking over. However, brakes steering and suspension, albeit in modified form, usually all came from the parent car, as did the engine, in the Ford's case an 1172cc, side-valve unit which remained in production for many years and was soon a firm favourite with the special builders.

Very few specials were built without any form of competition in mind, even if they did find their way on to the road. One marque which started out in this way was Dellow, the name derived from the proprietors' surnames, Ken Delingpole and Ron Lowe, who produced trials chassis to which customers could fit their own components or they could supply the running gear to Dellow for reconditioning and 'factory' fitting. The Dellow was introduced in 1947, not surprisingly for use with Ford Ten components, and it was so successful in trials that there was a great demand for a production machine. When Ford agreed to supply new parts to the company Dellow obliged and by the late 1950s the production machine was intended specifically for road use and had all the necessary creature comforts.

Over the years, the special has offered many attractions to the prospective sporting motorist: first, it can breathe new life into a car whose body is rusting into oblivion, but whose chassis and mechanical components are in a reasonable state; second, it is a cheap way of owning a 'new' car, in that second-hand running gear can be used; third, the egotistical owner can have a machine which attracts many curious, if not necessarily admiring, glances. After a boom period in the 1930s and 1940s, with a wealth of old Austin Sevens and Ford Tens to provide the necessary mechanical gear, the special seemed to be dying, particularly as in the 1950s trials cars needed to be more and more sophisticated in order to be competitive. However, there have always been a few companies offering new bodies to fit on proprietary chassis – although the steady ousting of the separate chassis frame by the unitary body has limited the choice of base car somewhat.

Towards the end of the 1960s, the platform chassis of the Volkswagen Beetle suddenly caught on as *the* basis for specials. It was possible simply to unbolt the body to leave a very handy and adequately strong floorpan, to which all the essential running gear remained fixed. This new awareness came first in America, particularly in California, where a completely new type of special was invented: the beach buggy. Designed primarily for fun use on the dunes in the warm Californian climate, beach buggies soon arrived in Britain, where they began to appear as everyday transport on the roads. On the whole, such vehicles were totally unsuitable for this use, often being equipped with second-hand racing tyres, of widths and constructions that endowed the buggies with extremely unpredictable handling on anything but the smoothest surfaces. Weather protection was usually minimal if it existed at all and the vehicles were often built in such an amateurish way that windscreen wipers and washers were considered an unnecessary luxury.

Regardless of all this, however, thousands of people found a great deal of enjoyment in owning a buggy and the cult slowly developed until some of the later machines were really quite refined and were often powered by specially tuned engines or even by the horizontally opposed six from the Chevrolet Corvair. Although the Beetle floorpan was used for almost all of them, it was commonly shortened by something around a foot in order to make the buggies more manageable on the bumps of sand dunes.

So the special survived – and continues to survive – with the Beetle turning into plenty of sleek, exotic devices other than buggies, the only fixed parameters being the chassis construction and the rear-mounted engine. The Triumph Herald/Spitfire chassis also provided plenty of opportunities for the special builder in the 1960s and 1970s.

There is a very fine line between this type of special and the more original kit car, although in theory the difference is that for the special the owner is expected to supply the base machine, while for the kit car it is common for the manufacturer to supply everything.

Like specials, kits were mainly a British phenomenon, particularly prevalent in the 1950s and 1960s. Their popularity arose out of a loophole in the British system of purchase tax, whereby this tax was applied to finished cars but not to their component parts. Not that much work often had to be done by the owner to complete the kit; a great deal of licence was used

here in defining a component car, so that at the peak of the kit car boom, towards the end of the 1960s, all that was necessary for the owner to do in many cases was to fit assembled engine, transmission and running gear units to a fully trimmed body or, perhaps to a separate chassis and then to the body. This tax loophole did have limits to its size, however; for instance, it applied only as long as instructions were not supplied with the kit! Enterprising manufacturers made short work of this, though: one printed a section at the end of the workshop manual for the car, explaining how to set about rebuilding the vehicle in the event of a total write-off; another seemed to circumnavigate the rule successfully by sticking instruction sheets for suspension assembly underneath the relevant wheel arches.

Sadly, the introduction of value added tax in Britain put an end to all this fun once and for all. This controversial tax was applied to motor vehicles no matter what their state of completion, so the one bonus of this type of component car had gone. Unfortunately, several of the kit builders disappeared almost with the old purchase tax; they could not build complete cars efficiently enough and in numbers large enough to offer them at prices competitive with those of the bigger organisations. One might expect that a kit should be cheaper than a finished car, regardless of tax, but in fact the amount of work that went into the kits was just about as much as into complete cars.

One of the first manufacturers of complete car kits was Buckler of Reading in Britain. For some strange reason, David Buckler's first offering was known as the Mark V and it featured probably the first multi-tubular spaceframe chassis to be sold commercially in Britain. The mechanical base was the good old Ford Ten, this being 1947, but many parts were modified and the two-seat glassfibre body was all Buckler's own work. Later cars were more advanced and were made to take engines from BMC and Coventry Climax, as well as Ford. Although some of the more than 500 Bucklers found their way on to the race tracks, these cars were always intended to be road cars. However, there were plenty of cases where kit manufacturers moved into that field from a beginning in racing.

By far the most famous example of this came

from Colin Chapman. The Lotus 6 was a simple, basic machine, but was primarily designed for competition use, for which it was ideally suited. After a highly successful four-year run, the 6 was replaced in 1957 by the Lotus 7, similar in concept, but more sophisticated in execution. This time glassfibre instead of aluminium was used for the wings and the front units were swept back rather than being like cycle mudguards. Lower and wider than the 6, the Lotus 7 handled even better and with power from any of a variety of BMC and Ford engines it was even faster.

Although it was fitted with a hood, and later models even had a heater, it was never possible to be really comfortable in a 7 in bad weather. Visibility was bad when the car was covered and anyone over about 5ft 10in tall was better off leaving his or her head outside. Despite all this, though, the 7 was probably the nearest thing to a single-seat racing car ever to be sold for serious road use. It became a cult car and went through four marques – the last of which had an all-new but unpopular glassfibre body – before Colin Chapman cried 'enough'. All was not lost, however, for Caterham Car Sales took over production, even reviving the old Series 3, and in 1980 the waiting list showed no signs of diminishing and this classic kit car lived on.

All Lotus's other cars of the early 1950s were built for racing, but at the 1957 London Motor Show Chapman took the major step of announcing his first closed car to the public – the remarkable Elite, otherwise known as the type 14. Not only was this hailed as a beautifully styled coupé, but it represented a major engineering advance in being the first car to have a glassfibre body/chassis unit. With Chapman's own design of rear suspension system – the Chapman strut – and a 1216cc Coventry Climax FWE engine, the little Elite was endowed with superb performance. It was a light car with a low drag coefficient, so although the engine produced only around 75 bhp the Elite could manage nearly 110 mph. Small modifications were required during the

The Lotus 7, still in production – in the hands of Caterham Car Sales – in 1981, went through a short bad patch when this Series IV glassfibre variant was introduced in 1970.

The first closed Lotus to be offered to the public was this beautiful Elite coupé, with glassfibre bodywork styled by Peter Kirwan-Taylor. Glassfibre also formed the monocoque.

car's life to improve such things as rear suspension location and body strength, but the Elite was generally accepted as being a fine machine and when it was replaced in 1963 its successor was greeted with a certain amount of trepidation. Chapman had originally intended to retain the glassfibre monocoque for his new sports car, but shortly before its announcement he realised that it would be a great deal less expensive to use a backbone chassis. This car was the Lotus Elan and it first saw the light of day at the British Motor Show in 1962. Not only did the separate chassis, which was itself remarkably strong, make the car cheaper, it also meant that a rolling chassis could be assembled before the body was fitted – the body again being a glassfibre unit. The lowly stressed nature of this meant that Lotus could produce the Elan in convertible form, something which had not been possible with the Elite, which required its roof for torsional rigidity. The general layout of the Elan was similar to that of the Elite, with independent suspension all round (although a lower wishbone was added to the Chapman strut set-up at the rear), but the power unit was based on the Ford 1500 Cortina engine and had a twin-cam cylinder head specially designed by Lotus. The original units retained the Ford's 1498cc capacity, but this was shortly increased to 1558cc and all the early cars were re-equipped.

If anything, the Elan's handling abilities exceeded those of its predecessor and the car was universally acclaimed as *the* sports machine of the day. Various models were built during the car's ten-year life; with varying states of engine tune; the final marque was known as the Elan Sprint and with a 126 bhp version of the twin-cam engine its performance was electrifying.

In 1967, a stretched and, if anything, even more stylish version of the Elan appeared, known as the Elan Plus Two and having two vestigial rear seats. Mechanically, the Plus Two was identical to the standard item, simply being based on a slightly lengthened chassis. Once again, however, it was available only as a fixed-head coupé. Lotus's final component car, which appeared in 1966, was the Europa, produced initially for export only. Again based on a backbone chassis, the Europa represented a new departure for the company in having its engine mounted behind the two seats. Originally, power came from a Renault 16 unit, but in 1971, by which time the S2 Europa had been on sale in Britain for three years, the Lotus-Ford twin-cam was substituted. The final version of the car, known as the Europa Special, had the Elan Sprint big-valve engine and an optional five-speed gearbox.

Sadly, value added tax changed Lotus's plans, as happened with so many other small manufacturers, and the company felt that if it was only going to build complete cars it should enter a different league. The new breed of Lotus cars which resulted, beginning with the four-seat Elite, was a long way up market from the earlier machines and ruled the marque out for many faithful followers.

One specialist sports car manufacturer with a long if chequered history is TVR. Like so many others, the company which launched the TVR name began in car production when the proprietor, then Trevor Wilkinson, decided to build a car for his own use. This was in 1947, the TVR name being extracted from Wilkinson's Christian name. Demand and the urge to be a car manufacturer prompted Wilkinson to take the enterprise more seriously and he began to fit modified RGS Atalanta bodies to chassis of his own design. It was the TVR coupé of 1956 which founded a family line still evident in the cars of 1980, although much modified. The basis for the TVR cars has always been a multi-tubular backbone chassis and right from the start independent suspension has been fitted all round. Engines for the early cars varied: some were Ford, some BMC, some Coventry Climax. As the 1960s progressed, however, the MGA engine became fairly standard. The United States had always been a major outlet for TVR and it was the frustration of an American owner, Jack Griffith, at not being able to obtain a replacement MG engine that led him to drop a 4.7-litre Ford V8 engine into his car. This was so successful that the company was soon listing the TVR Griffith as a production model.

In 1962, the company changed hands, and then again in 1965, having been placed in liquidation. The new owners, the Lilley family, set about organising the business properly and one of the early results of their efforts appeared in 1967.

In 1962, the Elan replaced the Elite and was made less expensive by the inclusion of this very tough backbone chassis, housing all the running gear.

Overleaf: TVRs retained the same basic body shape for many years and this body was shared in 1969 by the 1600 Vixen, shown here, and the 3-litre Tuscan.

Called the TVR Tuscan, this was basically an updated version of the Griffith, and initially its short wheelbase brought about extremely uncertain handling. Later in the year, the car was lengthened to put matters to rights and it was then offered with a 300 bhp version of the engine, which made it one of the fastest production cars in the world, with a top speed of more than 170 mph. Alongside the Tuscan came the Vixen, which was a Ford Cortina-engined version of the same car. The Vixen remained in production well into the 1970s, although the Tuscan was dropped in 1968 due to a shortage of engines. The name was revived in 1969 when the car was equipped with Ford's 3-litre V6 engine, but this did not offer the same type of performance by any means.

Nevertheless, steady development turned the Ford-engined car into a real winner and the late 1970s saw a turbocharged TVR for the first time, alongside an optional convertible. In 1980 a brand new model was launched – although still retaining the well tried chassis – and this was called the Tasmin. Still powered by the Ford engine, three versions of this stylish car were offered – open and closed two-seaters and a closed 2 + 2. TVR had certainly come a long way from its humble beginnings.

Two other small companies which built fine sports cars during the 1960s and 1970s were Marcos and Ginetta. The early Marcos cars of the late 1950s were ugly, if aerodynamic, creations resulting from a tie-up between proprietor Jem Marsh and aerodynamicist Frank Costin (hence the company name). However, it was the appearance of the Adams brothers as stylists which brought about the classic Marcos shape, which first appeared in 1964. This retained a plywood chassis, as first employed by Costin, but it was clothed in an exotic glassfibre two-seat body, whose sleek elegance the famous Italian styling houses might well have coveted. At the outset, a Volvo 1800cc engine was used, but this was replaced by a Ford Cortina unit in 1965, first 1500 then 1600cc, and a 3-litre V6-engined model came in 1969. Although strong, the wooden chassis took too long to make, so a cheaper metal frame was introduced later in that year. The final Marcos cars reverted to Volvo power, this time in the shape of a 3-litre straight-six, in deference to American regulations. The

introduction of a four-seater, the Mantis in 1970, was a disaster and the strain finally brought the demise of the company at the end of 1971.

The old story was true of Ginetta, the first such cars being built by the Walklett brothers for fun. Orders flowed in and the first important Ginetta was the little G4, which was designed to take a variety of engines and was offered in complete kit form; this model achieved considerable success in competition and with the similar G5 and G6 versions more than 500 were built. The direct replacement for the G4, and the most notable Ginetta of all, was the G15, which was a very pretty rear-engined two-seat coupé, taking its engine and much of the other running gear from the Hillman Imp. Available only in closed form, the G15 was announced in 1967 and remained in production until 1974, by which time the long-awaited G21 was finally on sale. Originally shown in 1970, with a choice of Ford 1600 or 3-litre engines and independent rear suspension on the bigger version, the G21 eventually went into production with a standard 1800cc Chrysler engine.

Also based on Imp parts – and one of the better kit cars – was the British Clan Crusader, which was announced in 1971. Unlike cars from many small manufacturers, the Crusader was built to a very high standard and was originally only offered in complete form, kits only coming on the market when sales were slow. Following Lotus traditions, the Clan had a monocoque glassfibre body, a very sturdy item which was not universally admired for its unusual styling. Well built the car may have been, but it was in direct competition with the Ginetta G15, although some £200 or £300 more expensive, and could not keep its head above water. Despite impressive results in racing and rallying in 1972 and 1973, these did not bring sufficient sales and in 1974 the company closed down.

Just as the small Hillman Imp provided a base for a few component cars, so did the ubiquitous BMC Mini. The attempts at utilising Mini components in specials of one sort or another were numerous and wildly varied. Some, such as the Mini Marcos and the Mini Jem, retained the Mini's component layout and simply substituted a new glassfibre coupé body, while others moved the engine to drive the rear wheels and revised everything else to suit. The most notable examples of this were the Unipower, a tiny but very handsome closed coupé of 1966, and the GTM, a similar type of car first seen in 1967. Neither of these was successful in the long term, but both were stylish and worked efficiently, the mid-engined layout giving superb handling and roadholding and the light weight offering surprising performance, even with the standard Mini engine.

While cars such as these strove to turn a common car into something special, a new business sprang up in the 1960s intent on reviving some of the so-called great cars of bygone years. These products were – and are – commonly known as 'replicars' and their quality has ranged from perfect in every detail to laughable. This type of enterprise knows no bounds of territory, manufacturers being rife throughout the world.

In America, the attempts have generally centred around earlier US models and there are a few notable examples. The Excalibur SS and SSKL machines were built by Brooks Stevens and his son David to resemble the similarly titled Mercedes-Benz models of the late 1920s and with Chevrolet Corvette power they were extremely fast. Cord and Auburn models also came in for the treatment, a company in Oklahoma offering a 7-litre Ford-engined copy of the 851 Speedster, known as the 866, and a less-impressive version of the Cord 810. There was also the Glassic, which was a glassfibre car, powered by an International Harvester four-cylinder engine and based on Ford's Model A.

In Britain there was a Bugatti 35 replicar from a company called Dri-Sleeve. This car, known as the Moonraker and powered by a Ford Cortina engine, was let down somewhat by its totally unsuitable wheels. Jaguar's products have come in for copying. With the XK engine still in production in 1980 it has not been too difficult for more than one company to produce superb copies of the fine D-type, complete with high quality metal bodywork. The old SS100 is revered by sporting enthusiasts and Panther's J72, while not, admittedly, a copy, had all the style and flair of that machine together with exceptional quality. Panther specialised in the flavour of a period rather than exact replicas and while their De Ville reminded one immediately of Bugatti's rare Royale it had an identity of its own. One other high quality replicar to appear in Britain was the Bentley Donington which, although built on a 1950s/1960s Bentley or Rolls-Royce chassis, had all the looks and breeding of the legendary Bentley sports machines of the 1920s.

There are still a few concerns producing specials and kits of one sort or another, but by and large the majority of famous names have either moved on to greater things or have become part of motoring history.

Overleaf: one of the many 'replicars' popular in the 1960s and 1970s – the Dri-Sleeve Moonraker. This was a reasonable copy of Bugatti's Type 35.

IF ONLY...

In all fields of motoring, there have been some legendary cars, ones which have caught the public's imagination – perhaps by mechanical excellence, by sheer opulence or by nothing more than attractive styling. Equally, there have been cars which had a profitable life almost despite themselves; such machines have been rather ordinary, but have appealed to motorists, often because of their manufacturers' reputations.

The converse is just as true. Plenty of fine motor cars have failed through no fault of their design or construction; some have gone down with their skilled but unprofitable builders, while others have simply appeared at the wrong time or at too high a price to suit demand. It is particularly with specialised vehicles, such as sports cars, that this has occurred, because whereas a family saloon has become a necessity to many people a sports car has always remained a luxury.

There has been a fair sprinkling throughout motoring history of sporting machines which have achieved the status of production cars but which really should not have gone beyond the drawing board and were not redeemed by manufacturers' reputations or anything else. However, it is possible that those same manufacturers have made equally classic errors by shelving sports car projects which, to many people, had all the makings of winners. Fortunately many of these designs did at least reach the prototype stage and although no one can state with any certainty that any of them would have been a success these one-offs give a good idea.

The 1930s saw a fine example of a car manufacturer which tried desperately to keep up with the big-time Joneses while being little more than a small engineering company. London's

Previous page : the HK500 Facel Vega was the most classic of the bunch, with a Chrysler V8 pushing it to over 130 mph, but it could not keep the company going.

A Vale two-seat sports car of 1933. There was nothing wrong with the Vale except its price – the small company tried to compete with the mass producers and failed.

Maida Vale district was the home of this enterprise and it was from this that the Vale Motor Company took its name. In 1932, Vale announced a small, low-slung two-seat sports car, powered by a modified 832cc, side-valve Triumph engine. There was nothing wrong with the new Vale: it could manage over 70 mph and could boast fuel consumption figures of which any modern day manufacturer would be proud. In addition, the little machine handled well and could stop in an impressively short distance. Two versions of the car were available initially: a standard model and a slightly more comfortable de luxe model. Both of these were two-seaters, but the following year saw the announcement of a four-seater, known as the Tourette and selling at only £5 more than the de luxe.

Vale advertised their car as 'The hand-made car at a mass-production price' and it was the latter part of that statement which began the company's downfall, even at that early stage. It was one thing for the likes of MG, Riley or Singer to produce their sports cars at popular prices, but it was another matter for the likes of Vale profitably to match those prices. After all, mass-production prices were possible because of mass production itself: components could be bought more cheaply in bulk and finished cars cost far less when made on a production line. Vale's efforts were noble, but it soon became clear that with the best will in the world the company could never make profits on the sort of prices that they were charging for their cars. In any case, effective though Vales were as road-going sports cars, they were neither tall enough for trials nor fast enough for racing, so their appeal for enthusiasts was somewhat limited.

For 1934, larger, Coventry Climax, engines were offered – either four- or six-cylinder units – and the company even offered to put new engines in existing cars. Prices now shot up to a more realistic level, but even so the company required good sales to make these prices economical, and those sales were never really forthcoming. Few

Vales were campaigned regularly in competitions such as this London – Scarborough Trial of 1933, but unfortunately the cars were not really suitable for either trial or track.

cars were turned out after 1934 and in 1936 trading ceased, with only 103 Vales built in total.

At the other end of the scale in the 1930s was another British sports car, which was the result of a schoolboy dream. This was the Squire, which had first been planned when Adrian Squire was but 16 years old. The first car was produced in 1934, from a works, in Berkshire, near Henley, and its specification was impressive. Two chassis lengths were listed and in theory open or closed bodies were available, but it seems likely that all the production cars built had open two-seater coachwork. The bodies were all styled by Vanden Plas and the result was a low, sleek sports car, which must have been one of the most elegant, well proportioned machines of the 1930s.

The chassis of the Squire worked well, with its semi-elliptic springs and its enormous drum brakes, but it was in the power house that problems occurred. Squire had opted for a brand new twin-overhead-camshaft British Anzani engine of 1500cc which he linked to a pre-selector gearbox, making do without the clutch. There was probably nothing intrinsically wrong with the Anzani engine; its valve gear was somewhat noisy, but in standard form it worked quite well and turned out 70 bhp. The difficulties arose from Adrian Squire's determination to fit a supercharged power unit to his new creation. He wanted a car that not only looked better than others but performed better, so he fitted a Roots-type blower at the front of the crankshaft to boost the inlet tract to a pressure of 10 lb per sq in. Power went up to over 100 bhp, but this gain brought with it unreliability in the form of overheating and short-lived head gaskets.

Even so, this was not really the cause of the Squire's short life. The car was built regardless of cost and so it went on sale as just about Britain's most expensive sports car. Unsuccessful forays into competition hardly improved the image of the breed and the company was forced into voluntary liquidation in mid-1936, after only seven Squires had emerged.

We have already seen that World War II was responsible for the demise of a number of car companies; these were of differing sizes and died for various reasons. One such was the Atalanta company, which was based at Staines, Middlesex, England and began car manufacture

in 1937. Only a few Atalantas were actually sports models, others being saloons and tourers, but those that were built were attractive and worked well. The early cars were powered by Atalanta's own four-cylinder, single-overhead-camshaft engines, with three valves in each cylinder. Two sizes were offered – 1.5 litres and 2 litres – and they produced 78 and 98 bhp, respectively, in normally aspirated form. With optional Arnott superchargers, power outputs increased considerably. In two-seater form, the Atalanta could top 100 mph and with all-independent suspension, handling was quite up to scratch.

For 1938, a V12 Lincoln-Zephyr engine, of 4.3 litres, was added to the list and this gave even more performance, while costing about the same. Prices were realistic and reasonable and the cars would almost certainly have had a good future had the war not intervened.

When Triumph announced the TR2 in the early 1950s, it was soon clear that this was an efficient sports car. However, it was not universally considered to be the most handsome machine in the world. One concern which took the view that the Triumph could be improved was the Swallow Coachbuilding Company (1935) Ltd, which stepped into the shoes vacated by the old concern after it had become first SS and then Jaguar. Swallow produced a new tubular frame for the Triumph components and clothed this in a steel-and-aluminium body with smooth, flowing lines. In appearance, the Swallow Doretti, as the machine was known, was not unlike the Austin-Healey 100 and most of the cars were open two-seaters. Although the Doretti was more lavishly equipped and therefore more comfortable than the Triumph on which it was based, it was just about as heavy and so was no faster. The specialised nature of the Swallow added considerably to the price asked for the Triumph and so there were few takers, even in America for which the car was designed. Nevertheless, nearly 100 examples were constructed in the Doretti's short, two-year life between 1954 and 1955.

Also Triumph-based was the Peerless, launched in 1957 and using TR3 components in a four-seat body, initially of aluminium and subsequently of glassfibre. Although a high speed tourer rather than a sports car, the Peerless was light and so could manage more than

100 mph, with acceleration to match. The 'proof of the pudding' was in a reliable run at the 1958 Le Mans race, a modified Peerless taking sixteenth place. This certainly brought increased sales, but the Peerless was never quite well enough made to be long lived. In 1960, production ceased, but the car's designer, Bernard Rodger, formed a new company and sold an improved version of the machine, called the Warwick. This was certainly a better car, but perhaps the damage had already been done and two years later, despite the introduction of a V8-powered version in 1961, the company again closed its doors.

When Peerless disappeared in 1960, its Managing Director, John Gordon, went into partnership with Jim Keeble to produce a car under his own name. Jim Keeble designed a four-seater GT car, powered by a 4.6-litre Chevrolet V8 engine and with an impressive chassis specification incorporating such niceties as a de Dion axle and all-round disc brakes. In fact, the Gordon had a lot in common with the Peerless, but it was of a much higher quality and with a steel body by Bertone and a top speed of around 140 mph, it promised great things. However, it turned out to be far too expensive to produce in that form, so it never passed the prototype stage.

In 1964, a new Gordon-Keeble company was set up to put the car, by now bearing Keeble's name alongside Gordon's, into production. Glassfibre was used for the bodywork in order to keep the cost down, but no expense was spared in the appointment of the car and the asking price of £2798, with a 5.3-litre V8, was totally unprofitable. Even a substantial rise early in 1965 still gave an uneconomic figure and, despite the sale of about 90 cars, the company was forced to close down in May of that year. A few more cars were built under new ownership, but by 1967 the enterprise was dead. The Gordon-Keeble, when finally priced realistically, aimed for a luxury market that simply existed no longer.

France had its own equivalent of the Gordon-Keeble, although it was a little longer lived. This was the Facel Vega which, although it was slightly earlier that the Gordon, coming in 1954, shared the concept of a stylish and luxurious coupé body combined with a large American V8 engine. Unlike the Gordon-Keeble, however, there was more than one Facel model. The classic one was the HK500, a two-door coupé powered by a 6.3-litre Chrysler V8 and having a top speed of over 130 mph. Initially the HK sold briskly enough to keep the company solvent, although there was never a large market for motor cars such as this. The car was face-lifted in 1962, when it became known as the Facel II, but by

Possibly the first production Squire, photographed outside Adrian Squire's home. The Squire was built regardless of cost, but was not reliable enough for the money.

then the company had launched a new small version, called the Facellia and powered by Facel's own twin-overhead-camshaft, 1650cc, four-cylinder engine. Initial problems with this engine hit sales hard and a switch to a Volvo 1800cc unit did little to restore the public's faith, although the Facellia was sold at a very reasonable price.

The model was dropped in 1963, but by then it had crippled the company financially. A receiver had been appointed in 1962 to run the company, but despite bold efforts at reviving flagging fortunes by fitting a 3-litre Austin-Healey engine, the market, as Gordon-Keeble found, was fast disappearing and the company closed in 1964.

Styling houses, particularly Italian ones, every year produce a selection of one-offs based on the mechanical components of existing machinery, which may be mundane or exotic. To a large extent these are either impracticable pipe-dreams, in terms of production possibilities, or else they simply are not as good looking as the car on which they are based. In general terms, if a stylist of note comes up with a really promising exercise then he will find someone to produce it, even if only in very small numbers. For instance, the car which eventually became the Fiat X1/9 first saw the light of day as an example of Bertone's expertise on a stand at the Turin Motor Show.

The converse is often true of the prototypes produced by major manufacturers. Sometimes millions of pounds are spent on development of a model before plans are changed and the project is scrapped. On other occasions schemes advance no further than the drawing board or first prototype stage before the axe is wielded.

In the late 1960s and early 1970s, Daimler-Benz spent a fortune on the development of a series of smooth coupés, powered by various types and sizes of Wankel engine and fitted with such sophistications as anti-lock brakes. After a considerable amount of testing, both privately and in the hands of the motoring press, these machines were quietly put out to pasture. Maybe management were foresighted in this action, but what fine sports cars these Mercedes C111 machines would have made, with their top speeds approaching the magic 200 mph mark.

If this was an example of an expensive indulgence, then Rover's engineers gave us a fine instance of effective development at a low price in 1967. At that time, mid-mounted engines were uncommon in road-going cars, largely because of the loss of luggage space which was a usual concomitant. The problem fascinated Rover designers, who turned out a really practical sports prototype in this configuration. This was called the BS and it had the appearance of a conventional front-engined coupé although a third seat was actually squeezed in the back alongside the offset Rover V8 engine. The gearbox was mounted ahead of the engine and driven by chain which allowed the power unit to be low enough to allow normal rearward vision. Contemporary press reports praised the little car which, with its extensive use of existing production parts, could have been produced very cheaply. Even the somewhat angular styling was popular, although it too was the work of the engineers and not the stylists. Sadly, though, the BS was not to be. Rover decided that they did not want a sports car and this delightful little machine was condemned to the museums.

Fortunately, the history of sports cars is full of motoring gems and there are not too many 'might-have-beens'. However, it is hard not to wonder occasionally what would have happened if only . . . .

Like Facel Vegas, Gordon-Keebles were built with no expense spared and in this case were then sold at far too low a price to be profitable. This 1965 car was one of the last.

IN QUEST
OF SPEED

BDG 227B

For many people, a motor car cannot be classified in the sports category unless its performance is considerably better than that of the average saloon. Of course, this leaves plenty of scope for liberal interpretation, but nevertheless throughout the history of the motor car there have been certain manufacturers whose vehicles have been built purely for speed. In some cases, this quest has turned the products into mobile hazards, as their handling and braking has not been a match for the sheer straight-line performance. It does not seem so many years ago that car makers were striving to break the 100 mph 'barrier' with a production machine – indeed, somewhat optimistic claims and counterclaims were rife and it was the practice of some manufacturers to offer certificates or plaques with their cars to say that they had been tested at a certain maximum speed. In the 1960s and 1970s 100 mph became no problem to even fairly mundane saloon machines, whose handling was also improved dramatically. For many years, there was no further speed barrier which was close enough to be broken, although 150 mph became more commonly possible. Sports car development progressed regardless, although the number of manufacturers in this field was declining. Among the so-called elite, the claims began to reappear; the emergence of Lamborghini, especially, enhanced this public rivalry. It soon became a case of who made the world's fastest production car and by 1980 the 200 mph mark was only a little optimistic for some cars. There are some very interesting machines which have contributed towards this search for the ultimate in performance.

Most of the cars in this category have fallen into a price bracket which is only within reach of the rich, but until British Leyland took over and instituted new policies, Jaguar had a reputation for producing stunning motor cars at everyday prices. From the lessons learned with the racing C- and D-types and with the road-going XK series, the company had all the ingredients for a sensational new sports car in 1961 and nobody was disappointed when the E-type appeared. With the 3.8-litre, triple-carburettor version of the ubiquitious twin-cam XK engine, all-independent suspension, disc brakes and a beautiful, curvaceous, two-seat body, this new sporting Jaguar offered the company's traditional standards of appointment combined with breathtaking performance. The cars road tested by the press in 1961 were capable of more than 150 mph, but these were carefully prepared by the factory and were equipped with racing tyres, which offered reduced rolling resistance. Even so, there was no question that the E-type was a very fast car.

Two optional body styles were available: an open roadster, with an optional hard-top, or a fast-back coupé with a third, rear, door. Neither version offered a great deal of space for the passengers, but this and indifferent ventilation were mere niggles compared with the sheer joy of driving this beast. In 1966, a long-wheelbase version of the coupé was listed for the first time and this 2 + 2 featured two vestigial rear seats as well as more overall passenger space. The roadster, however, continued on the short chassis.

By this time the engine capacity had been increased, a 4.2-litre unit being fitted from 1964, together with an improved all-synchromesh gearbox. Although the new engine produced more power than the earlier unit, it was more restricted in its crankshaft speed, and maximum speed runs involved over-revving. This may not have been as popular as the 3.8 car, but the E-type went on selling well and with only fairly minor modifications until 1971, when a Series III version of the car was announced, using only the long-wheelbase platform and having wider track, with flared wheel arches to suit. By far the most important change, however, was the announcement of a new 5.3-litre V12 engine to boost the performance of the now much heavier E-type back to its original standard. In theory, the six-cylinder was still available alongside the twelve for a while, but it seems that no six-cylinder SIII cars were built.

Opinions of the new car varied, but there is little doubt that this was another fine example of Jaguar engineering. Sales continued into 1975,

Previous page : to many enthusiasts the best E-type Jaguar was the original, powered by the free-revving 3.8-litre XK unit. This roadster of 1964 was one of the last 3.8s.

but by then the company had decided to move into a different field with its closed XJS and this, the last real Jaguar sports car, was killed.

The AC Ace was an efficient and stylish roadster when it was introduced in 1953, but steady development work turned it into a really fine sports car by the time the 1960s arrived. By most standards of the day, the Ace was an extremely fast machine, with any of its optional engines; in its ultimate form it could manage more than 120 mph. However, even this was not enough for the likes of American racing driver Carroll Shelby, who devised a scheme to install a big American V8 engine into the Ace chassis. He approached AC with the idea and the company agreed to supply body/chassis units to the States, so that Shelby could fit the engines. The result was the phenomenal AC Cobra, which was first produced in 1962, with a 4.2-litre Ford Fairlane engine.

It became clear that the chassis was not really rigid enough to cope with the power of the V8, so strengthening was applied and at the same time suspension and steering changes were made to improve handling even further, while disc brakes were added to the rear wheels as well as the front to aid stopping. This was in 1963 and at the same time the 4.2-litre engine was changed for a 4.7-litre (289 cu in) Ford unit, producing 280 bhp. The performance of the Cobra was shattering, with a top speed of nearly 150 mph.

AC quickly realised how good the car was and put it into production for themselves, mostly under the name AC 289. It became so popular that all the factory capacity was taken up by building V8 cars and the Ace was quietly dropped in 1964. Not content with the remarkable performance given by the 4.7-litre engine, Shelby managed to squeeze the 7-litre Ford Galaxy engine into the Cobra's engine bay for 1965 and AC followed suit with the 427 in the following year. 160 mph became possible with this car, which could show a clean pair of heels to many of the exotic and far more expensive Italian machines of the day.

Production of the Cobra finally finished in 1968, after AC had rebodied the chassis with new coachwork from the Italian Frua concern to turn the car into the AC 428. There was no doubt that the 428 was an elegant car and it performed well,

but it did not have the character and sheer masculine appeal of the Cobra.

Italy is renowned as the home of the supercar, but there are different grades of supercar and in the early 1960s a sort of second division sprang up to build superb body/chassis units and power them with commonplace American V8 engines. One example of this was the Iso company, founded by the Rivolta family. In 1963, a young engineer named Giotto Bizzarini laid down a brand new chassis, to be powered by a variety of Chevrolet and Ford V8 engines. The specification was very impressive and with two-seater coupé bodywork, styled by Bertone, and a possible top speed of around 170 mph (Iso actually claimed 186, but this reflects Italian optimism), the Grifo, as the machine was known, was destined for success. A measure of the Grifo's popularity can be gained from the fact that the car remained in production from 1963 until 1974, when for other reasons the company was beginning to run into difficulties.

In the same league as Iso comes the De Tomaso concern, founded by an Argentinian racing driver called Alessandro de Tomaso. From 1959 until the early 1960s, de Tomaso devoted himself to building racing cars at his workshop in Italy's Modena district, but for 1964 the company turned towards road cars and produced an open two-seater called the Vallelunga.

De Tomaso's first supercar developed out of the Vallelunga idea. In 1965, Giorgetto Giugiaro, who was then working for Ghia, rebodied the Vallelunga, but the resulting car was noisy and came in for a lot of criticism. De Tomaso persevered, however, and in 1966 Giugiaro was set to work again and came up with a superb body to house two seats with a 4.7-litre Ford V8 behind them. This was called the Mangusta and with a five-speed gearbox, all-independent suspension and disc brakes it promised much. Although the Mangusta (which means Mustang) had a top speed in excess of 160 mph, its handling was a little suspect. However, this did not stop the orders from flowing in, particularly from America. De Tomaso was not one to rest on his laurels, though, and he employed an engineer called Gian Paulo Dallara to find ways of improving the breed. As it happened, Dallara quickly became involved in other projects, such as Formula Two and Formula One cars, but when he turned his attention to the Mangusta, he decided that it would be easier to redesign it completely and the result was the Pantera (or Panther) of 1970. With a modified chassis and different suspension, not to mention an all-new body, the Pantera handled much better than the Mangusta and impressed the public and press alike. Indeed the Pantera was good enough for Ford to buy the De Tomaso concern with a view to producing the Pantera as a follow-up to its road-going GT40. This was a short-lived arrangement, but de Tomaso continued undeterred and later took over the ailing Maserati concern.

The Maserati company had long had a troubled history when Citroën took control in 1968. It was during this period that two important cars came out of the Modena factory: these were the Merak, which shared its V6 engine with the unique Citroën SM, and the Bora, Maserati's first mid-engined supercar. Although the company had produced mid-engined racing cars before, its road-going machines had all been conventional in layout. The Bora was announced at the Geneva Motor Show in 1971 and like so many more recent counterparts it was a sleek two-seater GT, with a five-speed gearbox, all-independent suspension and disc brakes all round. In this case, power came from a 4.7-litre, four-cam V8 engine, which had been developed over many years as a racing unit. The power output in road trim was 310 bhp, which was sufficient to give the Bora a top speed of more than 160 mph. Handling and roadholding were well up to scratch and the car was luxuriously appointed, as one would expect from a manufacturer of this class.

It was 1971 that first saw the Bora and when the Citroën partnership broke up in 1973 the car's future seemed uncertain, but two years later, as we have seen, Alessandro de Tomaso bought the company and put both the Merak and

Carroll Shelby turned the adequate AC Ace into the exceptional Cobra and eventually shoe-horned a 7-litre engine into the chassis to create this brutish 427.

*Previous page : Maserati's fastest supercar of the
1970s was the Bora, the first mid-engined
Maserati. With a 4.7-litre V8, the Bora could
manage more than 160 mph.*

the Bora back into production. Indeed he made
the Bora an even more exotic machine by
increasing its engine capacity to a full 5 litres,
thereby pushing its maximum speed nearer the
170 mph mark. Unfortunately, the dreadful
pneumatic braking system inherited from
Citroën persisted, the pedal being no more than a
button on the floor and offering about as much
sensitivity as a brick wall. However, the company
was planning to replace this with a conventional
system so that stopping would become a little
more predictable.

It is argued by many, that Ferrari's last front-
engined car was their greatest yet. This was the
365GTB4, better known as the Daytona. Introduced in 1968, the Daytona was equipped with a
4.4-litre V12 engine which produced 352 bhp,
and it was clothed in what must be one of
Pininfarina's greatest creations – a body of
timeless flowing elegance. The chassis was based
on that of the earlier 275GTB4 and it retained
that car's rear-mounted gearbox, but there was a
multitude of detail alteration. The Daytona was a
very easy car to drive and its docility belied its
staggering performance; with a top speed of
nearly 180 mph, there was no faster production
car in the world. The vast majority of the
Daytonas built were closed coupés, but the
company did produce a few open roadsters,
which were possibly even more handsome.

By 1974, when the Daytona was withdrawn, no
self-respecting supercar had a front engine, but
by then Ferrari had replaced it with an all-new
mid-engined machine called the Berlinetta
Boxer. This was again bodied by Pininfarina, but
this time there was an aggressive purpose in the
shape rather than a classic beauty. Power came
from a horizontally opposed twelve-cylinder
engine, based on the Formula One and sports car
racing units, with the same dimensions as the
Daytona's V12. The power output was 380 bhp,
so the Boxer promised to be considerably faster
than the Daytona; not only this, but with its wide
wheels and tyres and race-bred suspension, its

handling and roadholding should represent a
substantial improvement. The Daytona was a
practical grand touring car whereas the Boxer
was a machine built for outright performance
without consideration for such niceties as
luggage space. To drive, the two cars were as
different as chalk and cheese and it was very
difficult to identify a preference; the Daytona
could find it in its heart to forgive fools, but the
Boxer demanded a high degree of skill and
concentration if it was to be driven safely at high
speed.

In terms of outright speed, it soon became
clear that the Boxer was no faster than the
Daytona, the wind-cheating shape of the older
car compensating for its power deficiency. With

Lamborghini making outrageous claims for their Countach, Ferrari enlarged the Boxer engine to a full 5 litres in 1976 and pushed the performance nearer to the magic 200 mph mark.

While Enzo Ferrari was still thinking in terms of front-mounted engines for his 'proper' Ferraris (the Dino, with its V6, did not count), Ferruccio Lamborghini set the world alight in 1967 by turning what to some people was an impossible dream into reality when he put his mid-engined Miura into production. This had started life in 1966 when a rolling chassis was displayed to the public for the first time; nobody believed that a small company such as Lamborghini would be able to turn this into a finished car, but Bertone came up with a superb body design for this two-seater and the car was soon the talk of the motoring press. The engine was a 4-litre version of the V12 previously designed by Lamborghini's Chief Engineer, Gian Paulo Dallara, who was yet to find his way to De Tomaso's door. This four-cam unit, with a power output of 650 bhp, was mounted transversely behind the seats of the Miura and drove the car to around 170 mph. The suspension could be set up by the factory to suit the individual

Perhaps the most elegant Ferrari ever built, the 365GTB4, or Daytona, was the last of the front-engined machines, but could hold its own against the more modern Boxer.

customer, so ride and handling were adjustable, the latter varying from adequate to extraordinary.

The appearance of competition at the end of the 1960s prompted Lamborghini to extract even more power from the V12 and the 370 bhp version that resulted could power the car to a 180 mph maximum, making it once more the fastest production car made. However, the arrival on the scene of Ferrari's Boxer in 1971 jeopardised this status and Lamborghini's response came in the shape of the dramatic new Countach.

Once again styled by Bertone, the Countach made no concessions to civilisation – it was a pure performance car with futuristic styling to match. It was originally intended to fit a 5-litre edition of the V12, which might have taken the Countach's top speed over 200 mph. However, the old faithful unit was used and even this, with the car's low drag coefficient, could wind the machine up to nearly 190 mph. The Countach behaved impeccably on the road, with its massive tyres and carefully set-up suspension, but there was storage space for little more than a toothbrush and the shape of the car even precluded the use of proper opening windows. Perhaps seekers after the ultimate were not interested in details like this, but Lamborghini's cars generally had a reputation for poor finish.

At the other end of the quality scale there have always been the products of Germany's Porsche company. These cars are renowned as being engineered rather than simply built. Part of the quality must come from the fact that Porsche does not often produce a brand new car. Rather, it carries out a policy of steady development over a large number of years. The prime example of this is the 911 series, which came to life in 1963 and culminated in the Turbo model first seen in 1974. In some ways, the Turbo had the appearance of a 'boy racer': wide wheels and tyres, flared arches and a rear aerofoil. However in this case the object of the exercise was functionality

With Lamborghini's Countach, the Ferrari Berlinetta Boxer, particularly this 5-litre version, represented the ultimate in sporting motoring in the 1970s.

rather than show. With its enormous low-profile tyres, the Turbo's grip was sensational and even the higher rearward weight bias did not create problems. The power unit was the usual horizontally opposed, air-cooled six, but in this case with a capacity of 3 litres and a turbocharger to boost the inlet tract to 1½ atmospheres. Unlike the already superb Carrera, which gave driver and passengers an instant kick in the back if the power was used, the Turbo would surge forward, like an electric train or perhaps a rocket, as the rising exhaust pressure built up turbine speed. The beauty of the car was that if driven gently the turbocharger would hardly come into play and the fuel consumption would be very impressive. What is more the torque band was wide enough to render the usual fifth gear unnecessary.

Strangely, the Turbo's speedometer ran out at 150 mph, although the car was capable of nearly 160 with ease. In sheer speed this car was little quicker than the 2.7-litre Carrera, but it reached that speed so quickly and effortlessly and was so stable when it arrived there that it inspired great confidence. Throttle lag was something of a problem, particularly for low-speed overtaking, so for 1978, the engine capacity was increased to 3.3 litres and an intercooler fitted into the rear wing to cool the fuel charge on its way to the cylinders.

In 1980, the Porsche Turbo was still going strong, despite the existence of the company's own, newer, 924 and 928 models. It was extremely expensive, but it was still setting standards of refinement for others to match.

Britain can still turn out its high quality sports cars and it can still produce the power units to match foreign competition. It was in 1970 that Aston Martin put its V8-powered DBS into production. Initially, this was produced alongside the old DB6, but financial difficulties hit the company in 1971, and, after a takeover, the Aston Martin V8, as it was by now called, was the company's sole product. The delightful four-cam engine had a capacity of 5.3-litres and was equipped with fuel injection, although this was subsequently dropped in favour of Weber carburettors. Aston Martin do not quote power outputs, but this car obviously had a healthy one.

The DBS was a four-seater two-door coupé with handling to match its 150 mph-plus performance. Furthermore, it was beautifully trimmed and finished. Towards the end of the 1970s, after yet another crisis and subsequent ownership change, the company revived a name from its history when it offered a tuned version of the V8 engine under the name Vantage. Suspension changes were made to the car, which also grew a front air dam to cut drag and lift. With a five-speed manual gearbox, the acceleration of the Vantage was astonishing. It was not a light car, but it simply raced up to remarkable speeds and could top 170 mph.

To take matters one stage further, the company fitted a twin-turbocharged version of the engine into a dramatically styled, gull-wing-doored mid-engined machine, with the sole aim of proving that they could do it. This was titled the Bulldog and was very much a one-off, but Aston Martin confidently expected it to manage over 200 mph.

In addition to the true road-going supercars, there have been one or two adaptations of racing machines. The most notable of these was certainly the Ford GT40, which in various forms won the Le Mans 24-hour race four times. The road-going version of the car was the Mark III and was powered by a 4.7-litre V8. Even in detuned road-going form the engine gave the car astounding performance with a top speed of more than 150 mph. It was originally intended that twenty road cars should be constructed, but in the end the total was only seven.

Despite fuel crises and economic depressions, there were still some manufacturers in the 1980s who were prepared to put performance first on their list of priorities and, more encouragingly, there were still plenty of people with the money and the enthusiasm to buy their products. Punitive legislation, particularly in America, had taken its toll, but it looked as though man's thirst for speed could not be quenched and the search for the ultimate would continue.

INDEX